Shells, Spikes
and a dog called Drummy

SHELLS, SPIKES
AND A DOG CALLED DRUMMY

Five extraordinary years
in the life of an ordinary man

George A. Gregson 1914–1919

The War Diaries excerpts are Crown Copyright, use of which has been enabled by the Open Government Licence Version 3.0.

The Lancashire Fusiliers Annuals excerpts are used by the Permission of The Fusilier Museum, Bury, Lancashire June 2020

Copyright Michael Wilson © 2022
except where otherwise credited

Published in 2022

All rights reserved
Unauthorised duplication contravenes existing laws

Every effort has been made to trace the copyright holders and obtain permission to reproduce this material.

The right of Michael Wilson to be identified as the author of this work has been asserted in accordance with the Copyright, Designs and Patents Act 1988

British Library Cataloguing-in-Publication data
A catalogue record for this book is available from the British Library

ISBN: 978-1-3999-1554-0

Designed and typeset by
Carnegie Scotforth Book Production

Printed and bound by Totem

Strong, fierce like the mighty frightening war!

*Soggy, wet, pouring rain while the loud bangs and booms,
the sounds of guns and screams!*

All tense, with fright and might, ready to destroy,

*Yet, in the end there is hope and light, they may all live peacefully
with happiness and hope, that they live good lives together.*

Adele, 11, Great Grand-daughter, Poem Project at Primary School, 15.10.19

Lest We Forget

Those mentioned by name in George A. Gregson's recollections who died in the course of the war

Pte Tom Cowley, Lancashire Fusiliers, Warrington, U/K
Pte Danny Hodson, 1st Bn Lancashire Fusiliers, Colne, Gallipoli
Lt G. G. Needham, 1st Bn Lancashire Fusiliers, Werneth, Oldham, Hill 10 Cemetery, Gallipoli
Pte Lew Knowles, 1st Bn Lancashire Fusiliers, Suvla Bay storms, Gallipoli
Pte Paddy Murphy, 1st Bn Lancashire Fusiliers, Suvla Bay storms, Gallipoli
Pte Eddy Hills, 1st Bn Lancashire Fusiliers, Suvla Bay storms, Gallipoli
Pte Bernard Caine, 10th Bn Lancashire Fusiliers, Widnes, Arras Memorial, France
Lt-Col Bertram Best-Dunkley VC, 2/5th Bn, Lancasters, Pilckem Ridge, Belgium
Lt Bingham, 10th Bn Lancashire Fusiliers, Greenland Hill, France
Lt Hastings, 10th Bn Lancashire Fusiliers, Greenland Hill, France
Lt Knight, 10th Bn Lancashire Fusiliers, Greenland Hill, France
Lt Thomas W. Pollard, 10th Bn Lancashire Fusiliers, Greenland Hill, France
Lt E. H. Fryer, 10th Bn Lancashire Fusiliers, Guillemont, France
Lt Young, 10th Bn Lancashire Fusiliers, Warrington, St. Omer, France
Lt Sisson, U/K, Bethune Cemetery, France
Capt H. M. Adcock, 10th Bn Lancashire Fusiliers, Fricourt, France
Lt 'Rochdale', 29th Division, Lancashire Fusiliers, North of Arras, France

Private 6555 G. A. Gregson,
4th Battalion, Lancashire Fusiliers – Barrow Garrison

Lance Corporal 6555 G. A. Gregson,
1st Battalion, Lancashire Fusiliers – Gallipoli

Sergeant 5169 G. A. Gregson,
10th Battalion Lancashire Fusiliers – France & Flanders

Temporary Company Sergeant-Major 89672 G. A. Gregson,
4th King's Liverpool Regiment – France and Flanders

Contents

Prologue	xi
PART ONE	1
Pre-War	3
PART TWO	25
Training in Barrow August 1914	27
PART THREE	39
Gallipoli July 1915	41
PART FOUR	71
Rehab back in England January 1916	73
PART FIVE	81
France & Flanders May 1916	83
PART SIX	155
Staying on 1919	157
ADDENDA	187
List of Subscribers	216

Prologue

You would hope that everyone loves their Grandpa.

Did I love my Grandpa? Well, I never really thought about it. He was 73 years old when I was born and I was one month off 16 when he died.

He visited us regularly and often stayed over for extended visits. The Grandpa I knew was a very gentle, very quiet, calmly self-contained man who loved going to watch his grandsons play sport.

He'd had a son, Bernard, and two daughters, Monica and my mum, Hilda.

Grandpa loved his sport, particularly athletics, cricket and, befitting of a Widnes man, rugby league. He would come up to the Fylde coast to visit us, wrap himself in his big coat and sit in the front of my dad's car and watch. Indeed, when it was cricket, he would also meticulously record the score. And, I mean, meticulously. With a scrap of paper and a pen, he would score accurately each and every ball, dot ball or wicket, he would do it properly, he would do it right.

I have since learnt that 'doing it right' and certainly 'doing the right thing' went to the very heart of everything my Grandpa stood for.

In 2017 and 2018, my parents died.

My brothers and I were left with the memories of two happy and fulfilled lives. We were left with a couple of properties, many 'things' from furniture to artefacts to jewellery, and we were left with documents, news clippings and photographs.

The properties were easy to dispose of. No particular emotions stored in them as they weren't former family homes. The 'things' were a bit harder to sort out, most were donated, a few with particular memories attached to them were split between the brothers and their children.

However, the documents were a lot harder to deal with and within the documents were memoirs, photographs and medals from Grandpa's experiences in World War One.

Family legend has it that Grandpa saw a documentary on TV about the war and pronounced that something they were broadcasting did not happen in the way they said it did. 'I know because I was there.'

This prompted him to write these memoirs, we believe when he was about 78 in 1967. He referenced a diary that he wrote at the time of the war and a book where he recorded his athletics results. I have not been able to locate either of these records.

Grandpa fell into the classic 'never talked about the war' stable. But we all knew he had been through the war because we witnessed his recollections. We heard it at night as he dreamt the worst of it for the rest of his life. Grandma could not get away from the torment and his tortured memories.

I have one particularly vivid memory, near the end of his life, when I was revising for my exams not too diligently in front of the television and I witnessed Grandpa fast asleep on the settee putting a gun together. I watched confused as the gentle, kind man that I knew, efficiently assembled the gun.

My mum loved him with all her heart to her dying day. She survived dad by 12 months and, in those last months as the effects of an Alzheimer's diagnosis became more prevalent, her stories jumped 65 years to her youth in Warrington. She would talk about 'dad' and, initially, I would be thinking of my dad, her husband of 61 years but the stories were of her dad, my Grandpa. When she talked about 'home' she was referring to 365 Wilderspool Causeway, my Grandpa's house rented from the Greenall Whitley Brewery and the house she had left 62 years ago. That was his impact on my mum.

I then came upon the exercise book containing Grandpa's hand-written memories. A difficult read because they were written in capital letters with little or no punctuation. However, instinctively I knew it was an important read.

After a couple of false starts, the memoirs were given over to Sarah Stevenson and Lynne Fudge at The Fusiliers Museum in Bury. Lynne, as a volunteer and an absolute star, spent 15 months trying to find spare minutes on each and every Monday to commit the papers to a hard drive. To Lynne, we are most, most grateful.

Upon reading the resultant document, I was determined to edit the text in a more consumable format. It seemed like 'doing the right thing' for a man who was driven to do the right thing.

I have cross-referenced Grandpa's memories and, in this edit, have added excerpts from the Battalion's War Diaries and from the Lancashire Fusiliers Annuals with the intention of providing a context and additional dates for Grandpa's war. I hope these additions also paint a broader view of the war and make matters more vivid for the younger generations in Grandpa's family.

In a couple of cases, I have moved stories around to maintain integrity with the official records of what happened and where. An example is the Barny Caine story that I relocated after discovering his date of death through the Commonwealth War Graves Commission. I hope I have judged these 'moves' accurately, though I still have a little niggle about one or two.

I am certain that not all of Grandpa's recollections are 100 per cent accurate but they are how he remembered them. I am very happy to receive any comments about the story, in particular relating to historical accuracies. Please email me on Drummy1918@outlook.com.

I also hope my editing doesn't detract from Grandpa's story, I am fairly certain he would have forgiven me anyway given my motivation to do the right thing by his memories.

At this point, my thanks go to my wife, Jane, for her encouragement and wisdom and to my brothers and cousins for their support.

A very positive spin-off from these recollections has been the renewal of relationships with Grandpa's other grandchildren, my cousins. There has never been any falling out just life and distance getting in the way. I am particularly grateful to cousin Anne Wright who also had written notes of Grandpa and shared them with me. These added some critical times, dates and names that anchored some of the stories. Most importantly, the notes rounded off the 'dog called Drummy' story wonderfully. I am also thankful to cousin David Escott, an ex-Services man, who was able to provide valuable corrections and insights.

Further thanks go to my friend and ex-Director at Penguin Books, Mark Barrow, for a very early read (or should that be 'slog'?) and a good steer in the right direction.

And as you will see, Grandpa's story wasn't just on the battlefield but on the running tracks and cross-country courses of the North-West of England and France and Flanders.

We chose to donate Grandpa's service medals and the medals he won from his athletic exploits in the war and they can be seen in the archives at the Fusiliers Museum in Bury. We are grateful to Philip Mather, the archivist for all his support.

I have not been able to record Grandpa's writings word for word but have tried to be faithful to his story even where my understanding diverted from his writing.

I have researched further into Grandpa's pre-war cross-country career. He competed in the National Championships in March 1913 and March 1914 moving from 62nd to 25th. Part of me thinks that the war robbed him of his best years as an athlete, at a running distance that usually favours those in their late 20s. However, after reading his account, I can't overlook that his running ability played a significant role during the toughest five years in his life. Indeed, it undoubtedly gave him status, notoriety, won him friends, gave him income and, possibly, and I am guessing here, gave his senior officers an incentive to protect him from the very worst of the war. Well, it made his officers some significant cash. I could be wrong in this assertion as Grandpa certainly experienced the war at the sharp end.

Grandpa, you were a very determined man, you planned meticulously and loved getting a job done and getting it done correctly. I believe you were respectful to your senior officers and the army but you would dig in your heels and stand your ground if you were presented with a wrong that you could put right.

I can understand the trauma and sleepless nights riddled with nightmares. Yes, Grandpa, you had these but after reading your notes and after reading of others' experiences in those trenches, I now also understand the utter weariness at the end of it all. To survive Gallipoli, only to then have to go through France and Flanders, I can now identify with the need for peace and quiet and a simple life. I can imagine that you wanted for nothing more than to keep your head down.

Thank you, Grandpa, George Alfred Gregson, for a truly remarkable story and I'm sorry we never got to talk about it when you were alive.

PART ONE

Pre-War

Running for fun and marching for food

I, George Alfred Gregson, also known as 'Alf', within my family, and 'Greg', within the army, was born on the 5th November 1889. I attended two schools, West Bank and the National, both in Widnes, Lancashire (as it was then, now Cheshire). When I was old enough, I joined the Boys Brigade, the 1st Widnes St. Mary's West Bank group.

It's funny how life can turn on such small things but my membership of the Brigade would result in one very significant moment for me 26 years later.

Our Brigade captain at the time was the Reverend Corlett. We had two parades a week, on Tuesday and Thursday from 7pm to 9pm in the dining room of Gossage's soap works, kindly lent to us by Colonel Winwood Gossage who also contributed towards our annual camps.

These camps lasted about ten days each year when we would visit either the Isle of Man or Wales depending on where the boys voted to go. Three or four mothers would come with us depending on the numbers going which would typically be 30–40 or even more.

Ramsey, on the Isle of Man, was our favourite and where, one year, I won everything that I could on the sports day, the 100 yards, 220 yards, 880 yards, the one mile and then, in Ramsey baths, the swimming handicap beating Alf Lloyd into second place.

The four Gregson brothers swam in that race, Bob, Rafe, Ted and me, Alf. Our captain that year was Mr Joe Owen. He got me a gold medal that I gave to my youngest sister, Etty.

The camps were happy days. We just had to find the pocket money so the more you saved, the more you had to spend. On one camp in Ramsey, we had enough funds to go on the boat excursion to Belfast from Douglas and calling at Ramsey.

We marched up the pier which, incidentally, was built by the 'Foundry Company of Widnes' and when the ship, Mona's Isle, came along, we got onboard. The weather was hot, it was the first week in August and the sea was calm just as the doctor ordered.

There was just one problem, our two trunks packed with salmon, cheese and tomato sandwiches and cake were still on the Ramsey Pier Head and we were half way to Belfast with an eight hour stay on shore.

I had been called to blow the fall-in. I was sergeant and a bugler. When it was discovered no one had put those trunks on board, one grand gentleman, a Manx man, asked us to give a concert and he would sing. So, we started with band marches and community singing and the gent sang 'My old shako tin' in a lovely falsetto.

The gent told all the passengers of our predicament whilst we marched and did gym with relay races. He started a collection and went round himself collecting. The captain of the ship said he would give us all he could and he could get more when they reached Belfast.

When all the lunch had been served, we were able to go down. There was plenty of bread, butter, cheese, corned beef and cake and also plenty of tea and a little bit left over when we paid the bill.

We were collected at 10pm back at camp after a beautiful day. You will hear later of people saying that they were bad, old days but not with people like that knocking about. When I left the Boys Brigade, I was a Lieutenant.

Starting Work

Upon leaving school, I started work at JW Towers Chemical Apparatus Works in Croft Street, Widnes. I delivered orders out to all the works in Widnes, Ditton, Runcorn, Weston Point, Salt Union and Cashners. We were supplying acids (nitric, sulphuric, hydrochloric) and ammonia in Winchesters and we supplied all sorts of glass tubes, pipettes, beakers and other such products.

It was 1904 and I worked there for twelve months for five shillings a week, before, in 1905 and for six shillings six pence, I got work in Gossage's saw mills department.

My Uncle Jack Myers worked there also. He was a bad-tempered man who was always rushing. After a month or so, trouble started when Uncle Jack promised to put his clog to my backside.

Three other lads and myself were competing with each other to grab trolleys to get the wood that had been sawn into a lift to be sent upstairs. I was assigned to Uncle Jack and he expected me to grab every trolley as it came back down in the lift. One could easily get caught beneath the lift. If you dashed in too early your foot could get trapped between the bottom of the lift and the bed. One youth did get caught and was crippled. Horace Marshall suffered a crushed foot and limped for the rest of his life.

The trolleys were hard to come by and, some days, they didn't get emptied straightaway upstairs. Four went up and only one came down. The trolleys had long handles and three wheels with flat bottoms to place the cut lengths on and, when full, the trolleys were sent upstairs in the lift for the men to make soap boxes.

One morning, Jack was particularly agitated and Charlie Gill on the next saw told him to calm down.

I wasn't getting the trucks fast enough for him but he kept on sawing, pushing his lengths down the bench and every new cut was knocking the next one in line onto the floor. So, I sat on the timber and told Uncle Jack to 'get a move on'. That did it, he came round to kick out at me. I dodged him and grabbed his clog, lifted it up and down went 'gentleman John' (my mother's pet name for Uncle Jack). He was taken to the first aid station.

The first aid man came and he was actually my brother-in-law, Councillor (and latterly Mayor) Hesketh.

I was sent upstairs to Mr Dodd who was in charge of the box shop. I told him everything and Charlie Gill also spoke to him. Mr Dodd asked me if I would go to another department and I said, 'Yes, get me away from that madman.' I was sent to the boiling house in Mr Duxbury's soap-making department.

I started work there straight away with Jack Bell, a youth from Hale Bank, Ditton. I had to 'scuffle' the floor after resin, coconut oil and palm oil had been spilt from around the salt pans. At times, I got sent upstairs to the mixing room if Fred Baker or Amos Viggers, both Hale Bank boys, hadn't come into work.

Sometimes, Fred Baker would work upstairs in the mixing room until 3pm and then come down to help us in the boiling house. Fred was a good swimmer and was a first team polo player for Widnes Swimming

Club. Joe Peers was captain and club champion. Fred and I became pals and he got me to become a member of Widnes SC which I really took to. I won three or four prizes including a six large bottle, silver cruet set.

But I wanted to Run

I went to see Jack Frame of Gossage Street, Simms Cross, Widnes who was the secretary at Farnworth Harriers. The club had seen better days when Jimmy Hosper, Billy Mercer, Paddy Brady, Hughes, Flynn and Ince used to run.

Jack told me that if the club carried on for six months it was about all the club could do as it only had about ten members and three committee members. We wore a black vest with a yellow diamond and 'FH' in the centre together with white pants.

I joined and in the first novice race, came second behind John Watts to get a silver medal and then, at a later run, I won a first novice gold medal.

When we went to St. Helens to run against their athletic club, we had just three runners and two committee members, Jack Frame and Bill Joynson.

The publican was vexed, 'I have provided for a party and just five turn up!'

Jack told him how things were and he got into a temper.

'You should have written and told me you had called it off.' Not likely, 'We can lick all you lot with our three, that's why I brought them. Our three against your team, first three to count.'

Now, I had never had a bet in my life but when Jack told me that we had been written off, I was determined to. Jack said, 'Don't bet if you feel you shouldn't.' I said, 'No, Jack, put it in with yours. We'll show them.'

I was the 'novice' as both Tommy Turton and Jim Leadbetter were seniors. Well, I ran as if my life depended on it, 26 Saints versus 3 Farnworth Harriers from Widnes. I took the lead, going out of Knowsley Park onto the main road and never lost it. We had 1st G. A. Gregson, 3rd T. Turton and 4th J. Leadbetter. We got eight points to St Helens' thirteen. Point made.

We also won £2 10 shillings so we bought all the meat pies, ham sandwiches and Eccles cakes the publican had bought to sell.

Jack Frame was pleased and the publican was decent and made hot coffee.

He said, 'Not a bad novice, Gregson.' Jack said, 'Well, he's on form early.' Jack never said to me 'You're good' just 'always improving!'

You never got swell-headed with Jack. 'Wait until the others try,' he would say! But I liked Jack. He and his brother, Bob, both worked in the blacksmith shop at Gossage's. Old Mr Frame, their dad, was foreman pipe fitter also at Gossages. Arthur 'Chick' Johnson, the Widnes and Great Britain international Rugby League player (or 'Northern Union' as it was known then) also worked for Jack as a youth.

Farnworth Harriers finished the season and Jack told me to go and join a junior club as he thought it was too early for me to join the senior ten-mile cross-country races.

The first race of next season was the mile race in the Widnes Athletic Sports in June. I ran to orders. 'Try and come fourth, just out of the prizes just to see if someday you could do better.' He spoke like a dad would. As it happens, I had to try and win.

In the race, two bends from home, I glanced round, the third man dropped out and I was third and no one else was running. 50 yards away was the first man, 10 yards away was second. Jack Frame, on the last bend, shouted, 'Go all out, Alf.' I got second, twenty yards behind the winner without trying. It was a scheme that went astray!

My Widnes second prize was a case of six knives, six forks, six spoons and a neat three bottle inlaid cruet set that I gave to my mother.

The next race was at Warrington Athletic Sports. One mile and I ran second there and won a 4ft 6in hanging clock! Ernie Hesketh, the first aid man at Gossage's and my brother-in-law, was a joiner, he put the clock up for me at home in James Street, West Bank, Widnes.

When the Police and Tradesmen Sports came in August, I was trained and entered for the mile race. At work, I had seen Mr Duxbury and asked him to let me go at 4pm. 'Come to me at five to four, Gregson, and I will give you a pass to go out with.' He didn't give it to me until twenty to five. He had been detained at the General Office.

My race was at 5pm so I ran all the way to the Widnes football ground and got my clothes on. Jack Frame and his brother, Bob, were helping pin my number on. Out I ran at 5-1 bar on the betting. 'Critchley' the bookies shouted.

Mr George was the starter and he knew I was trying to win. He made it look as though he had a problem with his pistol and delayed the race by five minutes.

'You're late, don't do it again.'

He then whispered to me, 'Do you see that blue-vested chap, he is your rival here to win.'

It sounded like 4-1 and 3-1 was now being shouted for Critchley. Our people were 'in clover' as there were no bets placed on me because my number was twelve and I was in the centre of the field. When I got out of the tent, Jack knowing his bookie well (Berry of Liverpool, a reliable chap) took his money at 5-1. Just as he shouted '5-1 Bar', Critchley suddenly was laid at evens.

Mr George started us off. I was hemmed in so I took them by surprise and away I got after that blue shirt of Critchley.

Jack shouted at the corner where we would eventually sprint the last 100 yards. 'Don't overrun yourself.' I felt fine. I can still hear St Mary's Prize Band playing 'Caroline Brown' whilst we ran.

To cut it short, I passed 'Critch' round the second last bend on the popular side and came in first. Jack gave me an envelope to give to my brother Jim who was on duty, he was driving the bus.

I never knew how much was invested or how much was won at 5-1 but I know that Mr Duxbury's delay was a good thing for Jack and his brother, Bob!

I hadn't spent a penny on the race as I had only the time to put my running things on.

I do know the landlord of the Grapes was also happy as Jack took me to be introduced to him and I was welcome to the best drink in the house!

'Thank you,' I said and asked for 'a bottle of Cooper's lemonade, please.' And off I went with our Jim. When we had reached the town hall stop, I gave him the envelope with his winnings. Jack had already told him, 'Your Alf won' so he wasn't taken by surprise. All he had time for was asking what odds he had got. He was taken aback when I said it would have been 5-1.

When his shift was finished, he came home at 12 midnight and woke me up wanting to know all about it. 'A good night's pleasure and a £5 5 shillings gold chain,' was my reply.

So, I had won three prizes. Second got me £3 at Widnes, second at Warrington got me £3 3 shillings. The first, again at Widnes, was £5 5 shillings. £11 8 shillings in total.

Jack took me to the headquarters of the Runcorn Holy Trinity Harriers based upstairs at the chip shop near the canal bridge and I joined them.

We used to trot up and over Delph Bridge and start off to run round to the open country by the Norton water towers. Turning left to get on to the canal at Norton and a run home passing the gas works and finishing at the post office by the Delph Bridge.

Every Tuesday, Wednesday and Saturday, we trained. Thirty or so runners would turn up. Tommy Preece was there, he was the best runner and the captain.

When it got near the date for the Liverpool and District 7-mile Junior Cross-Country Championship, Jack said, 'Three more weeks to go now and I want you to get up to the front with all the leaders and stay there, though not necessarily winning the run.'

On Saturday afternoons, we ran 'friendlies' with clubs away at places like Runcorn, Warrington, Sutton, St. Helens, Makerfield and Northwich. Our last run on the Saturday before the big race was at St Austins H&A Club at Thatto Heath, round Rainhill way.

Jack said, 'It will have to be first today.'

Tommy Preece and I were running stride for stride. He had been coming in first in previous weeks but he couldn't get rid of me that day.

Wharton of St Austins was about five yards in the lead when we jumped through a hedge on to the main road to the finish at Thatto Heath, a mile or more away.

Tommy then tried to shake me off but I was running to orders, my best only would do that day. When Wharton spurted, I knew the finish was near round a bend 100 yards away and with the spectators waiting, I went all out twenty yards clear to win.

Tommy Preece always had his dad with him and he made the excuse 'Our Tom wasn't well today. Jack made him run out. It's next Saturday when he will have to do better.'

Wharton came along and said, 'Alf, you only need to run like you have today to win next Saturday.'

Wharton had won it in 1910, the year before, and he was running senior races.

Wharton said, 'I am running better and faster than last year. Today, round our regular course and no less or further than next week. We roughly call it our seven-mile course and today we knocked a minute off the best ever. So, next Saturday my bet is on Alf Gregson of Runcorn Holy Trinity.'

Jack Frame said to take it with a pinch of salt.

'Wharton isn't up against us next week. And he doesn't know what the other 150 runners think; ten or twenty must think they will win as they are running better. We should wait and see.'

On Wednesday night in the following week, Jack had arranged for me to run four and a half miles, from our old pub, on a measured road, run down Lowerhouse Lane to Farnworth Station Bridge, round Barrows Green to Cronton and then left turn, down past the cemetery, back past Widnes rugby football ground to Milton Road and back to the pub.

Jack was pleased. He said, 'Tired, Alf?'

I replied, 'I could have gone on but your Bob, by the football ground, told me to go all out. So I got tired quicker.'

I was always doing what I was asked to do. If Jack said 'do it' so I did it! He was always right for me.

Now, that Saturday's race was the big one at 3.30pm, seven miles from the Bebington showgrounds. It was the Liverpool & District Junior Cross-Country Championship.

The senior race was over and won by Chris Vose from Warrington Harriers who also won the team race.

Our seven miles was three full laps of the country course. We came into the showground, running up and past the stands three times then out on to the fields with jumps, water and the fields were ploughed aplenty.

I took a slight lead first time round. I increased it to twenty yards on the second lap.

By a hedge and near a farm, the farmer's family cheered me on, shouting and waving. It bucks you up on the last laps and I was still leading by 50 yards.

I looked for them and shouted to them, 'It's the last lap now.'

The farmer said, 'Well get a move on' just when Bob Frame would have said it if he could have been there!

I got into the sports ground and we had to run one lap of the ground and go over to the right.

Each lap we ran through, I could see the number of the last man and I could see all who followed Tommy Preece who was second, 150 yards behind me.

Runcorn Holy Trinity didn't finish a team as only four out of the ten needed for a team ran the race. The other teams were able to pair up going into the second or third lap.

I won.

Tony Wharton was one of the first to congratulate me and he was excited. Jack soon had me in the dressing room as Tony would never stop talking.

'Alf, lad, you can catch cold by standing there. It's cold and windy weather. Let's get you dressed quickly and I'll go and see Berry.'

When I got there, Berry shook hands saying, 'It's a good hiding I should be giving you, young fellow. You have taken all I had taken and a bit more! I send it on to Jack with pleasure.'

Jack said to me, 'You can take your Jim's.' That was the second time I took Jim's.

I had won £1 10 shillings at 2-1.

It was another day to remember, they were happy days. I got a gold medal given by the Evening Express Newspaper 1911, it was a lovely design.

Meanwhile, back at work

I left Gossage's to work in my dad's shop in West Street, Widnes. I was repairing boots so I didn't find much time to train in the summer. I would keep training up, on the grounds of Widnes Cricket Club.

Mick Gildoly was groundsman. J.O.W. Twist took us for sprint training, us being Tommy Turton, Paddy Blinstone, Tom Albert, Alf Burgess and the 'Brothers from Mersey Road' (that is, where my brothers and I lived at the turn of the century and how we were known).

Jack Frame was still looking after my running. He never married so did what he pleased as regards hobbies. Jack told me to go and join Warrington Harriers and Athletics Club.

That winter I was busy in my dad's boot repair shop when Alex Bailey called one Saturday afternoon at 2.30pm. He asked dad if I could go over to Runcorn and run for Warrington Athletics Club. Dad was pleased to think Warrington could do with me but I wasn't keen. I hadn't done any distance running since the Liverpool race. Mother told me to go home to James Street and 'get your bag packed and off with you.'

Alex came with me making sure I went over to Runcorn. They were running a friendly with Albert Farrel's Runcorn Tally Ho Harriers which included Albert and Jack Dutton both running. They were first and second always for Runcorn. It rained all day and in the fields there were many savage pools of mud. The tins of water after the race were not too warm and in that dressing shed, there were a few draft holes!

I finished third behind Vose and Holbrook, both Warrington runners. First, second and me in third so Warrington got a surprise.

Not much attention must be paid to friendly runs though especially for speed because the best runners like to get in condition slowly doing the distance for staying power. Then, they start speeding up nearer the proper race time.

Warrington AC wrote a nice letter to my parents, it was from Charles Berry, the Secretary of Warrington Harriers and Athletics Club.

'They would like your son to join the club.'

They also thanked Mr Gregson for allowing his son to run on Saturdays knowing it was his busy day at work.

'If Alf wants to come to train the nights are 7pm Tuesday and Thursday and 3pm on Saturdays from our Fletcher Street headquarters alongside Warrington Football Club.'

I went over on the next Tuesday with Tommy Turton and Alf Burgess. I had been to Gossage Street on Sunday to tell Jack Frame about Saturday's run. He wasn't surprised, 'Turton and Burgess would have put them up to it.'

Warrington AC was a club with such internationals as Chris Vose, Herbert Holbrook, Billy Bolton and Frank Antrobus, runners who were picked many times for England. Sixty runners would turn up for training where our expenses for rail fares were paid together with supplies of embrocation, hot water, towels, soap and tables for rubbing down and massage. If you wanted to keep a club with good class runners and you wanted to keep them, then you needed to encourage them.

I was later offered work at A.W. Howard Estate Agents in Legh Street, Warrington, where Charlie Berry (Warrington's Secretary) worked. We talked it over at home and the family decided it was more money for me and the Co-op had opened up a few doors away. Mum and Dad thought that the Co-op would put grocers, boot repair shops and others out of business.

Sadly, it did.

Dad was asked to repair shoes, boots and all sorts but the Co-op meant our shop went bang like some others. 'The small honest man goes under.'

'We are for the working man,' said the Co-op. Not in cases such as these.

Moving On

I eventually moved to live at 107 Slater Street, Latchford. The home of Mr and Mrs McKean.

Fred Shadwell, who was a runner and bicycle racer, working then at the saw mills at Crossfield Soap Works, was also living with the McKean's. Later, Fred opened a motor repair business in Lovely Lane and, subsequently, with his sons, a coach business, Shadwells Coaches of Warrington. I was good mates with Fred until he got married to Rose.

The McKean family took me on as one of their own. Fred, Charlie (the grocer's manager at Cross's) and I were just like brothers and we were all runners.

Hilda, the McKean's daughter married Jess Russell who worked as a manager at the Walker's Brewery. Maggie, the McKean's other daughter, married Tom Gee, a blacksmith at the Vulcan, Earlstown.

I was one of them, nothing was too much for them, it was home from home. I could fill a chapter with their kindness that they showered on me.

'Anything in particular this week, Alf? Perhaps a dance? When lad? Tuesday, Thursday or Friday?'

I shared a bedroom with Charlie until he married another Rose (Harper). Well, on my bed would be white shirt collars (glossed), underwear and socks. There would be dance shoes with a lovely shine on them, patent ones.

I went out as nice as any boy would like to be. And I wasn't courting. No, I was free to pick and choose or leave alone.

Later, I had taken to a young girl and went about with her. I couldn't get on with her mother. I liked her dad, but not her mother or two sisters! The girl's mother was telling me I should pay a bit more attention to her younger daughter! I won't say who the family were, it will be best not to.

Well, our club, Warrington, were bent on sweeping the board in both senior and junior races.

On 15th February 1913, The West Lancashire Cross-Country Championship was to be held at Scale Hall Farm, Lancaster.

So, I was hard at it. Tuesday, Thursday, Saturday and other nights, training. Walking on Monday, Friday and Sunday mixed with a bit of courting.

The 15th February came and on that Saturday morning, I got to Bank Quay Station, Warrington, to find my eldest brother, Jim, already there.

I introduced him to Warrington AC's champion, Chris Vose. Chris would eventually represent Great Britain at Antwerp in the 1920 Olympic Games. They travelled together which was just the thing as Chris wanted someone new to talk to.

The night before, my brother had packed up taxi driving for Connors Taxi Cabs, on Sankey Street, and I didn't know then that he intended to go to Canada. Our Jim only talked when I asked him something.

'Hello Jim, you coming to Lancaster?' I asked him. 'Yes, it's time I saw you run for the first time.' Jim and Chris both walked up to Scale Hall Farm together.

When we got to the dressing room, Chris said, 'You have a nice brother, Alf.'

'Yes, Chris, and there's four more at home!'

'I hope he has luck when he goes to Canada.'

I was taken aback.

Well, in short the senior ten-mile race was over. Chris was first and Herbert Holbrook, also from Warrington AC, was second. Our senior team won the race.

It turned out that Chris told Jim if he wanted to win big money he could start taking bets, taking one bet at a time.

Chris told him to, 'Start with our crowd betting on Joe Hanson to beat your Alf. Don't take a bet on your Alf, not one. Your bets will cover if it doesn't come off.'

Joe Hanson was from Warrington AC also and there were plenty of bets on him.

Now, the morning papers had all plumped for Joe Thompson from Lancaster which was the local club. Jim took a lot of money at 2-1. At 3-1 were Albert Farrel from Runcorn and three or four other runners from Sutton, Ravenhead and Wallasey. All the clubs and their supporters backed their best runners at 4 or 5-1.

The junior race was three laps, seven miles in all. It was up and down with hedges and jumps and a downhill finish of 800 yards.

On the first lap, I was boxed in a corner going out into the country and was 15th. Jack Frame who was there shouted to 'Increase slightly, Alf.' On the next lap, with our Jim and Chris, Jack shouted, 'Get going you have four to beat and you are lagging by 100 yards.'

Billy Bolton, the international, was waiting half way round that last lap waiting for me to come, just a mile from the end.

'Greg, get it over now, don't leave it for a sprint!'

Jack Battersby, one of our committee men, shouted 'Go, Alf, now or you have had it.'

I reached Joe Hanson and kept on at my pace. He had to spurt to keep me back with 250 yards to go.

Charlie Berry and Alex Bailey shouted but I don't know whether it was intended for my club mate Joe Hanson or me.

I felt I could keep on so I spurted and went all out, not worrying whether he came back at me or not. I got home first and Joe came in second. According to our official times in the Warrington Guardian, I finished in 41 minutes 15 seconds and 23 seconds would be the difference at the end between Joe and me. It had been a gruelling seven miles across country with jumps, water, brooks, ploughed fields and hills. 23 seconds would amount to 120 yards.

Well, my brother Jim was all smiles.

'I turned bookie, Alf, and got a clear book thanks to you and Chris

Vose. Chris told me my brother, 'With a good try, will beat them all today.'

Just three weeks later, Jim did emigrate to work with cars in Saskatchewan, Canada. I never knew what he cleared that day in Lancaster and I didn't ask him.

It was at Bank Quay Station, Warrington that I gave him my winners gold medal on the £5 5 shillings gold chain.

He didn't want it, 'No, Alf, no.'

I replied, 'Look, I want you to remember me sometimes so, when you look at it, I know your thoughts will be on the day your passage was paid to Canada by those that had no faith in me! Not like Vose and you.'

We didn't realise that Jim would soon be back with the Canadian Forces fighting in France.

Now, I ran in a couple of sports meetings trying the 880 yards or 'half-mile' as it was popularly called. I did fairly well coming 5th and 4th.

In 1921, I also competed in the Northern Cross-Country Championship at the Aviation Racecourse, Doncaster. It was ten miles with 36 obstacles and two miles of ploughed field and I finished in 66:26, in 14th place behind the leader who finished in 62:39.

In both March 1913 and March 1914, I competed in the National Cross-Country Championships at Dunstall Park, Wolverhampton and at Chesham respectively. I had moved up to senior racing in both events and improved from 62nd to 25th in horrific conditions in the space of 12 months. I was now beating some very good runners.

I completed the 8.5-mile course at Wolverhampton in 54:48 (the winner won in 51:02) but the course should have been ten miles and we didn't know it was short when we were running. Chris Vose came second and, according to The National, would have won it if it had gone the full distance. We came second as a team at Wolverhampton.

At Chesham, I did the ten miles in 76:14 (the winner finished in 70:26) and Warrington were the 7th team in. The conditions at Chesham were definitely a pre-cursor of what was to follow in my time at Gallipoli and France and Flanders.

August 1914 arrived and war was looming.

Grandpa, the runner, in Warrington AC colours

Warrington AC 1913. Grandpa is 4th man in from the right on 2nd row down (standing). Note the three England internationals sitting around the shield with the red rose on their vests. Olympic Games athlete, Chris Vose is the man with the moustache and the other two are either Herbert Holbrook, Billy Bolton or Frank Antrobus, all internationals selected from the Warrington club.

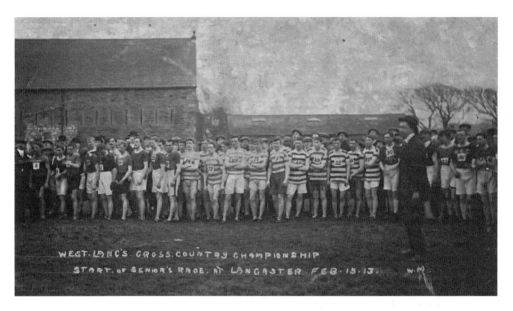

Runners lined up at the start of the West Lancashire Cross-Country Championship at Lancaster in February 1913

Warrington AC runners at the line up of the Junior race at the West Lancashire Cross-Country Championship at Lancaster in February 1913. From left: 37 J. Watson 28 Grandpa 29 J. Hanson 36 W. Walters 31 J. Nurse 38 H. Woods 33 N. Stafford

Chris Vose, Olympic Great British athlete at Antwerp 1920, and Warrington AC team-mate and the man who told Grandpa that his brother, Jim, was emigrating to Canada

Grandpa with Joe Hanson, both Warrington AC runners, who came in 1st and 2nd respectively in the West Lancashire Cross-Country Championship at Lancaster in February 1913

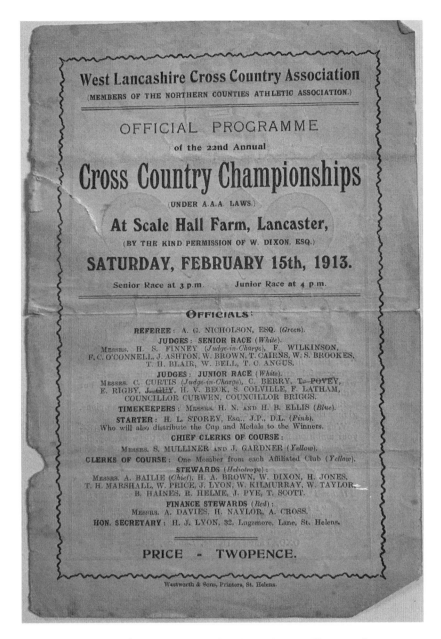

The programme for the West Lancashire Cross-Country Championships 1913

Overleaf: the programme for the Liverpool & District Championship in 1911. Grandpa ran for Runcorn Holy Trinity Harriers and won the race

5 ST. AUSTIN'S H & A C
(Thatto Heath)
Colours—Dark Blue Singlet, with Light Blue Trimmings.

- 60 Jaques, W
- 61 McDermott, J
- 62 Mercer, E
- 63 Mercer, P
- 64 Pimblett, J
- 65 Rigby, H
- 66 Rigby, W
- 67 Reynolds, J A
- 68 Waine, R
- 69 Wyatt, T
- 70 Woods, W
- 71 Wharton, W

Reserves:
- 72 Connor, T P
- 73 Grundy, R
- 74 Woods, T

6 ST. HELENS PARISH CH. H
Colours—White. Badge—P C H C

- 75 Barton, A
- 76 Curran, J
- 77 Greenall, J
- 78 Grundy, A
- 79 Hilton, R
- 80 Illingham, J
- 81 Roughley, J
- 82 Slater, W
- 83 Slocombe, H
- 84 Twist, C S
- 85 Waring, H
- 86 Welding, J

Reserves:
- 87 Scott, J
- 88 Mustard, J

7 ST. HELENS REC C & A C H
Colours—Cardinal Singlet; White Knickers.

- 89 Anders, E
- 90 Brown, J
- 91 Innes, D
- 92 McGurk, W
- 93 Marsh, G
- 94 Marsh, J
- 95 Owen, F
- 96 Shevlan, C E
- 97 Swift, J
- 98 Stott, J
- 99 Topping, J
- 100 Wilson, W

Reserve:
- 101 Cathcart, J

8 SOUTHPORT H & A C
Colours—Navy Blue.
Badge—Large S in Gold.

- 102 Bennett, H
- 103 Clayton, A
- 104 Clayton, R
- 105 Gardner, F
- 106 Lamb, C
- 107 Fraser, J W
- 108 Newton, T
- 109 Pounceby, G
- 110 Pounceby, A
- 111 Symons, N
- 112 Taylor, F
- 113 Wilson, G

Reserves:
- 114 Mac Cave, J
- 115 Webster, J
- 116 Brooks, H

9 WALLASEY A C
Colours—Green Singlet; White Knickers. Badge—W

- 117 Baker, L D
- 118 Bale, E S
- 119 Brookes, T J
- 120 Figueiredo, E
- 121 Hughes, T M S
- 122 Plant, E
- 123 Scoins, A G
- 124 Scoins, H R
- 125 Scott, P
- 126 Spence, C H
- 127 Thornton, F L
- 128 Young, R

Reserves:
- 129 Lowes, R G
- 130 Spence, G H

10 WATERLOO H & A C
Colours—Blue and White Hooped Singlet.

- 131 Drennan, H
- 132 Finerty, J
- 133 Finerty, P
- 134 Gannon, T
- 135 Gormley, M
- 136 Johnson, G
- 137 Lonsdale, H
- 138 McAffrey, T
- 139 Parker, H
- 140 Plint, J A

GRAND FOOTBALL MATCH.

WEST CHESHIRE LEAGUE. Div. I

Bebington St. Andrew's (GREEN)

v.

New Brighton Tower Amateurs (RED AND WHITE STRIPES).

Kick-off, **3-30** p.m.

REFEREE – MR. A. PERCIVAL

Every Competitor must wear complete clothing from the shoulder to the knee, viz.:—sleeved jersey and loose drawers. Unless so attired, no Competitor will be allowed to compete.

NOVICE CHAMPIONSHIP.

At 3 p.m.

DISTANCE—About 6¼ miles.

One lap on Track and Four Circuits over the country, passing through the Grounds each time.

RULE 19—Teams.—That not less than six or more than twelve members compete from each club. The first six of each club to count, and the club with the smallest aggregate to be declared the winner.

PRIZES.

First Team ... ... Six Gold Centre and Enamelled Medals and to hold the "Courier and Express" Trophy for twelve Months.

Second Team ... ... Six Silver and Enamelled Medals.

First Man Home *Alf Gregson* .. Gold Medal.
(Presented by the Proprietors of the "Courier and Express.")

First Man Home of an unplaced ⎱ Gold Centre and Enamelled
Club *Tom Preece A.* ... ⎰ Medal.
(Winner outright excepted.)

ENTRIES.

1 L,POOL ODDFELLOWS H & S.C.

Colours—Blue Singlet, White Knickers. Badge—Crimson O.

1 Brown, W 7 Kay, W
2 Chown, W C 8 Kernigham, H
3 French, R 9 Marsh, W A R
4 Higham, H 10 Mason, W H
5 Higham, W 11 Robinson, L
6 Kay, J 12 Smith, J

Reserves:
13 Ellis, J   14 Morrison, W
15 Levens, V

2 RICHMOND H

Colours—Claret with Blue Facings; Black Knickers.   Badge—Large R.

16 Adams, T 22 Jones, E E
17 Aird, W 23 Kersey, W
18 Ball, J A 24 Middleton, A J
19 Black, D 25 Molyneux, T
20 Fry, E B R 26 Rowan, D
21 Hughes, W 27 Turner, A E

Reserves:
28 Kersey, A E 29 Handley, J
30 Marsden, H

3 RUNCORN HOLY TRINITY H

Colours—White Jersey; Blue Knickers. Badge—R.H.T.

31 Banner, J 37 Mattravers, H J
32 Cashin, G 38 Preece, A T
33 Curzon, L 39 Pollitt, L
34 Greest, H 40 Street, N
35 Gregson, A 41 Williams, H
36 Jones, T 42 Yarwood, J

Reserves:
43 Cashin, H   44 Layland, A

4 RYLAND'S WORKMEN'S REC. CLUB (Warrington)

Colours—Blue Jersey; Black Knickers. Badge—R.W.B.

45 Brookes, F 51 Hollington, G
46 Brookes, W 52 Welsby, H
47 Barton, E A 53 Whitmore, A
48 Cotton, A 54 Warburton, T
49 Eckersley, J 55 Warburton, J
50 Harding, C A 56 Wood, H

Reserves:
57 Green, P   58 Noons, T
59 Hesketh, W

PART TWO

Training in Barrow August 1914

War is on – best do something about it!

August the 4th 1914 and Britain had declared war on Germany. On Sunday evening about 6pm on the 9th August, I decided it was time I did something about it.

Mr McKean got up, all 6ft 2in of him, put his pipe away, came to the couch and asked, 'Alf, you not going out tonight? You have not been to Bank Park with the boys to hear the band.'

I replied, 'No, I am going to sign up in the morning.'

'Can't you leave it a while? It's early yet,' Mrs McKean tried.

It was no use. I had made up my mind. Mrs McKean said quietly to her husband, 'Edwin, why don't you go? You have a good shot.'

'Yes', and looking over his glasses at me said, 'yes and so have the other buggers, Alf.' That stuck with me many a time in the months after.

Next morning, I got to the offices at A.W. Howard and waited for the office to open. I told Charlie Berry and also George Nelson that I was joining up like others in the McKean 'family' such as Bobby Hewitt.

Some of my mates were going to wait as they all seemed to think the Germans would pack up at any time. I got home to Widnes, told dad and he took it very hard. Mother, without breaking down, said, 'You are old enough, not like our Bob. Be on your way Alf, your two youngest brothers, with Paddy O'Neill, have already gone twenty minutes ago.' When I got in the room, my brother Bob was going over to Runcorn.

Rafe, at seventeen, was actually three months too young and Bob was only sixteen but, I tell you now, Bob got in the Navy and, after training, worked on HMS *Dreadnought*!

Rafe, Paddy O'Neill and I had to pass the Doctor at Warrington Police Station on Thursday at 10am. I wasn't superstitious but it was the 13th.

We cleared the medical, then the Inspector took our names and details such as our dependents, single or married, religion and then they asked one more question, 'Army, Sea or Air?'

'The Lancashire Fusiliers' was entered so we went from Bank Quay Station to Bury, the headquarters of the Lancashire Fusiliers.

We were put in tents and given two blankets each. We put them down where we wanted to sleep that night. We strolled round and at 12.30pm went by the cookhouse.

A rough looking chap was sat with his back against the cookhouse wall with a big Dixie by his side. He had a bone and was picking the meat off. 'Come on, help yourself, you're in the army now.' We selected one each and picked it. It was good but I was not used to eating like that.

We got to the gates and asked the Sergeant if we could go into Bury. 'Yes, be back if you want some tea by 4.30pm prompt.' We were sat down on the blankets when two Lancashire Fusilier soldiers came with a Dixie of tea and bully sandwiches. There was one mess tin between three. So, we did all right and they came back to see if we wanted more of each.

At 6pm, a bell sounded to fall in. We got down to the square. The Sergeant wanted 200 men for now. Paddy and my brother Rafe said they didn't fancy night travel. I didn't mind, it was just the same war whether it was night or day. So I fell in, marched to Bury with four Sergeants including Sergeant Guardsman Keegan, Sergeant Bamber, Sergeant Mellor and a fourth Sergeant whose name I have forgotten.

That simple decision split Rafe and me up. Rafe joined the 12th Battalion Lancashire Fusiliers and went off to Salonika. He returned to France eventually as part of the 6th Battalion.

I was now Private 6555 George Gregson, he was Private 6556 Ralph Gregson.

Training Begins

According to the Lancashire Fusiliers 1914/1915 Annual, the 4th Battalion Lancashire Fusiliers *'arrived on the 9th August 1914. The base was shortly inundated with large drafts of men from the Depot, which brought the numbers up to 2,000 men. The men were mostly in civilian clothes, not the best, an excellent indication that the nation meant to win this world war at all costs.*

There was a lack of rifles and clothing.

On 18th August, the Battalion HQ and five companies moved from the Vickers factory to Cavendish Park, the home of the local cricket club, accommodated under canvas.'

We arrived at Barrow in Furness at Cavendish Park, the home of Barrow Rugby, the Northern Union (re-named in 1922 'Rugby League') team and it was also the Barrow Cricket Ground.

Some soldiers were put into tents and some into the football pavilion. Again, we were given two blankets. The next day was spent in forming a company.

Our company was G Company and our Company Sergeant Major was CSM Donovan, "Irish", loaned from the East Lancashires.

The Sergeants worked overtime getting us into four platoons. I was in No. 2 platoon reporting to Sergeant Bamber who was also on loan from the East Lancashires. Next, we were put into sections, No. 8 was mine.

The Sergeants wanted a section leader for each section. Sergeant Bamber asked for old soldiers to step out. He selected four and placed them as section leaders. He was not satisfied with Bob Crompton. He was too nervy, too late with his orders.

Sergeant Bamber then said to me, 'I'll try you this morning' and I surprised him. 'Where did you learn all that from, as you already know?' 'The Boys Brigade,' I replied.

A day or so after, we had a young platoon officer attached to us in No. 2 platoon. He watched us drilling our section and called to me 'halt them!'

'What is your number?' '6555, Private G.A. Gregson' I replied. He responded, 'Well, tonight's orders will read Lance Corporal Gregson, Lancashire Fusiliers Corporal, an NCO (Non-commissioned officer).'

I was given a red tunic with one stripe on each arm and a cap.

Private Harry Gardner, Private Waddington and Private Jack Ratcliffe were the other section leaders.

The Lancashire Fusilier 1914/1915 Annual says, *'Early in September, the LF's (Lancashire Fusiliers) relieved two detachments of the 4th Border Regiment on Walney Island and acquired an excellent training ground.*

It continued, *'it was not until 17th March 1915 that the Battalion realised they were to become a draft-finding unit. Up until then, they had hoped to join the Expeditionary Forces as a unit. On the 17th, they were requested to* *send large drafts of officers, NCO's and men to the South Lancashire and East Lancashire Regiments.'*

Those regiments were not my final destination, a different future unfolded for me.

For now, we believed we would all be together as one unit for the Expeditionary Force. My company was G Company, 4th Battalion of the Lancashire Fusiliers, Cavendish Park, Barrow-in-Furness.

Our A Company went into hutments at Biggar Bank, two miles away on Walney Island. The C Company went to Webb's Farm, North End, Walney Island. It eased the pressure on space on the park. G Company, my company, was the last to be formed. If more recruits wanted to join the Lancashire Fusiliers, they went to Hull to join the 3rd Battalion.

Our G Company was made up of Captain Wilcox, our Commanding Officer. No. 1 platoon officer was Lieutenant McIver, No. 2 Lieutenant Ravenscroft, No. 3 Lieutenant Butler and No. 4 Lieutenant Garrett. As said, our Company Sergeant Major was CSM Donovan. I was in charge of Section 8, No. 2 platoon under Lieutenant Ravenscroft.

We were now preoccupied with drill, physical training (PT) and lectures. If it was wet, we filed into the big stand. Our lectures were mostly about rifle use, bayonet fighting, sights, finding targets to fire at 'actual fighting' distance (i.e. range) and direction.

Sergeant Bamber was a quiet person but thorough in everything he did. No. 1 platoon Sergeant Keegan, a guardsman on and off parade, shouted! He was smart. No. 3 platoon Sergeant Eccles, a typical Lancashire 1st Battalion man, he could be Keegan, Bamber and No. 4 platoon Sergeant Mellor, all in one. We liked Eccles's lectures. He kidded a lot. Just when we got excited with his stories he would put the dampener on it. If he did want to drive a point home, he would start with, 'Now you must pay attention, this is what you all will have to learn for your own safety and probably to save yours and others' lives one day.'

For PT, we route marched at night down to the targets at Roose (the Rifle Range), fired the course and did all the necessaries 'for active service.'

The Commanding Officer, Captain Wilcox, asked for anyone who had ever fired out of a rifle and about fifty men stepped out. Sergeant Keegan took charge of them and marched them off to a big hut. These huts were being thrown up day and night as tent sleeping was getting chilly by then. The fifty men (a platoon) got uniforms, rifles, full equipment and were drill-disciplined.

Private Tom Cowley, whose parents lived on Dalton Bank by the Rylands Wire Works in Warrington, was one of those fifty men. His brother, Bob Cowley, was in the Battalion orderly room. We saw that party march off one Friday night to Barrow Station and our Battalion Fife band marched them up.

The party had had about four months training as true volunteers and when they were asked, 'step out anyone who has fired a rifle' they had stepped out without hesitation.

It was three weeks short of Christmas 1914 but we did not know to which area they were going. Just after, we learned through Bob Cowley that their Tom had got killed.

Also local to me in Widnes and Warrington were Jack Ratcliffe, Bill Shinley (the Rylands Association plasterer), Jim Trotter, Bill Chesters (from Liverpool Road) and some others. I mention these, in particular, because I gave their families a visit when I was on weekend leave, and they tried to do the same for me.

We all delivered letters to each other's mothers or wives, children, other relatives and friends to let them know we were all right and we would take things back if they wanted us to.

We had been provided with everything a soldier required and did all the training like those brave fifty men did in October and November 1914 but we did have a longer time to do it in.

There was also a bit of excitement.

Back to what I love – running

On Friday evenings, always at 6pm, the Company orders got pinned up outside each Company HQ. One evening, it read, 'All interested in Cross Country, please turn out 3pm tomorrow Saturday on the parade ground in gym clothes. A three-mile run will take place, just for pleasure.' About twenty turned up including three Lieutenants.

It was a steady run. Lieutenant Ravenscroft was in charge, the officers in college or university costumes. It was a change and it was enjoyed.

We, in our Companies, did about a mile, a little over, every morning; they called it rouse and parade.

We would set off from the cricket ground through the small wood onto the main road then round the park, by the cookhouse and up to the start. Each man did that in two minute intervals and then roll call was over.

I loved it, a good wash outdoors followed with plenty of cold water. Taps were turned on and the water flowed into bowls then into a v-shaped trough to flow away. We shaved and then we were ready for tomatoes cooked with bacon and plenty of juice to mop up with your bread.

On Tuesday afternoons at 3pm, the same party that ran Saturday's fun race, turned out. We were all volunteers although you didn't feel like dropping out.

On Thursday and then Saturday, it was a four-mile round rouse. We got to look forward to it and we enjoyed it. One man, Private Merry, was very keen and would make sure he got on and finished fast along the sports ground cement track to our barracks hut finish.

I asked Lieutenant Ravenscroft what was behind all this running. I could understand the rouse parade was compulsory. He said the Commanding Officer knows that a seven-mile Barrow Garrison Cross-Country Championship was to take place but no one knew yet when. Each competing team would consist of ten runners, all ranks. Well, I told the boys and told them training would be stepped up bit by bit. Training would become a little longer and a little faster.

We got to know when the race was to take place, 3pm Friday. I was told to take over from now on.

Lieutenant Ravenscroft told me that I had to select the ten men and instruct them in so far as what was required of them. He told me the names must be in by 5pm on the preceding Saturday. They had to be sent up to the Garrison HQ on the Monday.

Twelve names could be selected but only ten to run as a unit with the top six to count for the team. The prize would be £10, £1 for each team member, if successful. The team that wins would get the lowest aggregate number of points for the first six to complete. The other four runners must also finish even though they do not count for the team prize. The army had its own rules and regulations as I found out later.

I needed to pick the best and couldn't pick an officer. The twelve that I selected were better at 'staying the pace.' I picked those who would stick it out as endurance was needed.

I told them to run in pairs and I said, 'Pick your own partner.' I wanted them to choose a partner who was about equal because I wanted them to finish the race and not to drop out. I told them they must not drop out of the race.

'So, I will expect you to come along in twos at the finish. Try to beat each other when you know it is near the finish because the more soldiers you all pass, the less our points when added up,' I added.

On the Saturday before the Friday's event, we had a training run.

Merry was, as usual, first by the bottom entrance at the cookhouse and there was about two yards between us. He glanced round and when on the track with 120 yards or so to go, he went full out. I still stopped two or three yards behind him as winning this race didn't matter. He was first.

Now I had to pick and, then, get them to state who their partners would be. I entered all the names down leaving Merry and me. I said, 'That leaves you and me to run together. I want our team to win more than I want the individual winner of the race.'

'Why should I have to stop with you? Every Saturday I have done but what's to stop me on Friday? No, I am going all out from the pistol start,' Merry stressed.

'Right, so long as we stick it out, that's what matters to me,' I replied. I selected the two best reserves, twelve had to be named so that if there was any change, such as one of the running ten took ill or had an accident, then one reserve could take his place. There were fifteen units entered with 150 runners needed to finish. Each 4th Battalion Lancashire Fusiliers Company, from A to G, had a unit entered as did the Borderers, the RFC, the Manchesters, RAMC (Medical Corps), RASC (Service Corps), the Engineers and the Lancashire & Cheshire Regiment.

We had our last run on the Wednesday afternoon at 3pm and practised Friday's route, we went from the cricket pavilion. It had a big clock and I noticed the exact time Friday's race was from the cricket ground.

So, we rehearsed it, through the woodland of trees and on to the main road, turned left, then turned left again into our camp by the main gate next to our guard room. The only exception is that, on Friday, we would turn right for Walney Island. We then ran our usual course.

I wanted to know how we felt as regards fitness. On Thursday, we all had a ten-mile walk, 10am to 12 noon followed by dinner and then afternoon bed, if you felt like it.

Our Captain had given me a free hand after Wednesday's run, walking was to take the soreness out of our legs. Our beds were made snug and warm by using our pal's blankets, under and over oneself. Regarding rubbing down, we had plenty of help from some boxers and wrestlers.

Luke Tierney, an old wrestler, was in charge but I had to stop him rubbing me as his grip was so strong. He hurt my muscles and I didn't want to be running sore. He was all right on the big chaps, plenty to grip to massage!

Well, Friday soon came and the run was started at 3pm by Captain Madeley, Adjutant of the 4th Battalion Lancashire Fusiliers.

Regimental Quartermaster Roddy announced the instructions for the race, 'Keep all signallers on your left, turn left through the gate on to the main road, next turn right to Walney Bridge which you must cross.'

I took the lead just round Vickers Corner turning to the right as I approached the bridge and came across a youth on a bike that looked like he was from the butchers. I think he had a basket on the front with parcels in. He got in front of me as I tried to go on to the bridge.

He almost stopped and I stumbled into the side of the bridge. Captain Madeley, after he had started the race, had followed us on a motor bike and swerved round. On seeing what happened, he asked if I was all right. 'Yes, Sir,' I said, getting into my stride while he caught up with the youth. There were now three runners in front of me.

I got up to the leader and could see by his running gear that he ran for some university or college with badges on his top, both back and front.

It was rather hilly from Walney Island to Biggar Bank. Half way up, I caught him but he kept me behind him. If I tried to go past him, he would speed up. When I tried at the right turn along the coast road, he looked at me. We were level and he meant to stop me.

At that turn, on the sandy beach by a shelter, I caught sight of red-caps with flag tapes and stakes at the finish. I knew it was about two miles to the village and back so I intended to get on with it or get beaten trying.

I gradually crept on fast, he still tried and I spurted at the turn. We had to turn right on to the top of the sand hills running parallel with the coast road. I could see the others following to the village.

I had just got on top when our postman, Corporal Harry Howarth from Horwich ran up the sand bank and ran in front of us by a couple of yards. I shouted for him to drop out as it could get me disqualified if it was considered as 'assisting.' However, he wouldn't pack it in so I got desperate and tripped him from behind. Down he went, I jumped over him and on I went the final 800 yards to win by 80 yards.

The Borderers Captain spoke to me at the finish. He thought it was funny to see the Corporal roll down the bank. He said, 'You didn't need help. He hindered you, not helped you.'

We chatted until the General presented the prizes. He congratulated me and I refused the £3 10 shillings money and only accepted the gold medal. He said, 'You are all right Lance Corporal Gregson, winnings from army running do not disqualify you from amateur sports.'

'I should like something for that amount,' I replied. 'So you shall, Corporal' and he asked for G Company's Captain to come forward. When he sprang up to attention and saluted, the General told him to look after 'his champion, a good runner.'

Private Merry finished as our second man, his position in the race eleventh. When we got back to camp, Merry said, 'Corporal, you must have been pulling my leg.'

A week later, I was presented with a semi-hunter silver watch to the value of my prize money. This watch is now in the Archives at the Fusiliers Museum in Bury.

The Captain said, 'The chain is also yours. Your Lieutenant's bought it for you and the Captain has got it inscribed.'

On the back of the watch, around the edge, it read '5169 Lance Corporal G. A. Gregson 1st in The Barrow Garrison 7-mile Race 1915.' In the centre, the letters 'G.A.G.' (George Alfred Gregson) were interlocked. The date was 15th April 1915, just 10 days before the Lancashire Landings at Gallipoli.

Lancashire Fusiliers Annual 1914/1915 says, *'the Battalion ran quite successful association and rugby teams. An inter-unit cross-country run* called for some strenuous training on the part of Company teams. We managed to get the first man home, but secured only second place in the team competition, the Lancashire & Cheshire RGA (T) being the winners.'

Back to Business and off to war

The Annual continued, 'Soon after June 1915, the Battalion lost Sergeant-Major Cox who hurriedly joined the 1st Battalion as Quartermaster.'

Well, the war was still on and I was in Sergeant-Major Cox's footsteps.

Our Company got put through its paces, 60 NCO's and men. We received 48 hours home leave, having to return on Friday night.

Finally, we were marched to Barrow Station and travelled all night down to Devonport (Plymouth).

It was a long night but no sleep would come as we wondered where we would land. We knew it wasn't France.

I thought of Jack Ratcliffe, Stanley Chesters, Bob Cowley, Micky Toghes, only two from the Warrington group were still left behind. One was Harry Gardner, a quiet youth whose father was a grammar school master. I would see Harry again in very different circumstances.

The other left behind was Jack Hague, a coal miner, from Ashton. He was Company Sergeant Major Donovan's No. 1 nightmare! Jack would never be what a Sergeant-Major wanted, he couldn't march, his arms always swinging together forward at the same time, his shoulders leaning forward, a typical miner.

He was upset when the time to say, 'Goodbye, Jack' came. I remember just after the race, the same General who presented the awards, held a general inspection as he wanted to see for himself the much talked of G Company with the 4th Battalion's best records. We were clean, smart and absenteeism was none.

Well, Donovan was watching us file out of our hut for the inspection and Jack Hague was just in front of me. Donovan got him by the shoulder and pushed him back in the hut. 'God!' he said 'book in sick and close the hut door.' Jack was happy that there was to be no parade for him. That was Jack Hague.

On another morning, it was raining and we had lectures in the hut and Donovan told us how cruel we would have to be when in conflict. At question time, Jack shouts "Dust yer think yer human?" That started it. He told Jack that if he didn't shape up when out on active service, he would be soon polished off.

'You're useless Jack', 'am I? Sithy mon, give me a pick and shovel I'd get more coal in 5 minutes than you would get in a 5 hour shift.'

'Yes,' Donovan said 'and you can have it, Jack lad. You are good there, old lad. I try to be good as a time-server and I like to give you all good advice.' Donovan continued saying, 'I'm not saying this to find favour or soft-soaping. I have never had a full company of men anything near like this G Company, from Captain Wilcox down to my nightmare Jack.' He marched out.

There was a boxing competition in the YMCA on the Friday night after the seven-mile Garrison race.

Lieutenant Butler, a young Barrow solicitor, happened to be a university boxer at heavyweight category. He got in the ring straight from his billet and didn't know that no one was due to box him; he must have frightened them all. Butler was tall, strong, very robust and fourteen stone.

Captain Wilcox, from the ring, announced that he was sorry that G Company had no one with guts enough to take on Lieutenant Butler.

'Hold on, Sir, hold on. We haven't got anyone in our Company anything like the Lieutenant's height and size but, if he wants to punish someone, he can have me to punch.' It was Donovan.

He took off his hat, tunic and braces and fastened them round his waist. He got some gloves put on by none other than Jack Hague.

Well, those three rounds were as good as I have ever seen. Lieutenant Butler tried to knock the Company Sergeant Major out but Donovan boxed him. He was as smart on defence as he was on parade. Donovan stood straight up with straight lefts going in time and again. Lieutenant Butler was 20 years old, Donovan was 40 and finished with not a blood stain. Butler's nose was like a red cherry and he got a cut eye-brow. The next day, he was wearing a plaster on it.

We thought a lot of the Company Sergeant Major that night. When we congratulated him next morning on winning, I said, 'You have boxed before, Sir?'

'Yes, when I was 24, I was the Light Heavyweight Champion, sixteen years ago.'

All kinds of recollections came to me on that train journey to

Devonport. We arrived into the big hall, got our meals and when we were given 'topees for the sun', we knew it would be the Mediterranean area.

PART THREE

Gallipoli July 1915

Off to the sun

We sailed at midnight in darkness. We called at Gibraltar, Malta, and Alexandria but we were not allowed off the ship.

According to official records, *Lance Corporal G. A. Gregson disembarked in the 'Theatre of War' on 18th July 1915.*

The official Lancashire Fusiliers War Diaries stated that on 20th July, *'200 reinforcements arrived at Lemnos.'*

We had Lancashire Fusiliers and all sorts of units including the Dublins, the Munsters, the Engineers, Gunners, REMEs (Royal Electrical and Mechanical Engineers), some nurses and there were guns. We got off at the Greek Island, Lemnos, and, in 24 hours, into motor boats with thirty men in each. Again, it was night time and we were getting nearer and nearer.

The War Diaries state that on 21st July, at 15:30, the men, *'embarked from Australian Pier – half the Battalion on board HMS* Bulldog *– destroyer & the remainder on transport. Disembarked on V Beach – Peninsula at 9pm. Marched to Gully Beach.'*

We started to hear gun fire, louder and louder. Then we got close enough to see some shells dropping into the sea. We steered a zig zag path.

It did seem ages before we, in a dozen boats, single-filed in semi-darkness up to a ship, grounded head on to the beach, it was a collier, the River Clyde. A big hole had been made in the stern. A platform hung down so we could step on to it and walk through the boat. We got the same way onto a pontoon, on to a low pier and to the shore.

Shells were coming faster but we, and the boat, could not be hit by those shells. The tall cliff was too high and a shell occasionally did hit the top of the cliff and sent rocks down. They would go 20 to 30 yards out towards the water.

It was hard work walking in twos up the silvery, sandy beach which smelt awful, of mule, horse and dirt. We moved on and got organised up along a rocky path. There was about enough room for a single cart only to travel up or down.

While we waited, we looked round the coast; the barbed wire reminded me of Warrington and Rylands Works. It was stacked up in heaps six or seven yards apart and four to five feet high. It was trip wire that the Turks had placed in the water and, when the landing took place, the troops got stuck fast on the spikes.

The troops got shot at on those very rocks that we sat on while waiting to move on which we eventually did, passing the Lancashire's cemetery. It was a bad start being a Lancashire Fusilier.

It was day-break and after sandwiches, bacon and tea, we reached the 1st Battalion Lancashire Fusiliers 29th Division Headquarters. We got divided into four sections and attached to a set of twenty or so men. Then into a communication trench seven feet deep and about two and a half yards wide. Of course, a good many like myself did the same but many, sadly, did a lot worse.

The Lancashire Fusiliers Annual said, *'On 21st July, The Battalion was hurried back to the Peninsula, as there was reason to believe that the enemy were contemplating making a heavy attack. This, however, did not come and after a few days at Gully Beach, the Battalion went into the trenches. Gully Beach, also known as Y2 Beach, lies some 2km north of X Beach and about the same distance south of Y Beach on the north side of the Gallipoli Peninsula.'*

I was part of B Company, No. 2 platoon 1st Battalion Lancashire Fusiliers. Our platoon officer, Lieutenant G. G. Needham, said he was short of NCO's (Non-Commissioned Officers). He would like me to accompany him at 4am in the morning. Having gone through the sailing, dodging shells, avoiding getting sunk, passing through that 'scented' sandy beach, passing the cemetery and everything else that day, I slept.

The Corporal on watch duty wakened me at 3.45am, told me to dress battle-order with rifle loaded with the safety catch on to 'make no mistake.'

I was ready, when the Lieutenant said, 'Come on, Corporal.' I had no idea where I was going, leaving our trench called Bond Street, into Trafalgar Square, under the Marble Arch, down Piccadilly and into Ludgate Circus. All these places had names put up on the side of the trenches and I suppose some Londoners had made those trenches and named them well.

We came to a low trench with no earth on top. It was newly dug, straight out towards the Turks, about 25 yards. It sloped up at the far end with branches and twigs over the end top. We stooped down.

Lieutenant Needham was behind me with my rifle. He was looking through his field glasses out in front. He gave them to me and I looked half right, 40 yards or less, 'you will see a Turk digging,' he said.

I got used to the morning mist and gloom and whispered, 'I have got him.' Lieutenant Needham aimed and fired, up went a pick and down went the Turk. He pulled me back. 'Come on out of here, Corporal, as fast as we can get.'

We rested in Piccadilly. Then the Turks bombed and, with machine guns, blazed away for half an hour. When they stopped, Lieutenant Needham said, 'You have had a baptism. You will do, Gregson. I'll see you later.' When he came, it was after breakfast. The first thing he did was to take up my rifle, examine it and look through it.

'I see you are a true soldier, he looks to his rifle first.' I was put in charge of No. 2 section.

He took me all along the front line occupied by the B Company. The trenches were well-built, clean and disinfected to help to keep the flies away.

When we got back in the support line about 60 yards back, I met one of our youths, Private Danny Hodson who was, like me, from Barrow and the old 4th Lancashire Fusiliers. In fact, I had been out at Barrow with him and his pal Private Billy Hale. They were both from Colne.

One night, Danny was in Dalton Road, Barrow, just ahead of Billy and me. Danny was thick set, 'tubby' and he turned around saying something I just couldn't understand in his broad Lancashire accent. 'What's he saying, Billy?" I asked as I could not even guess what was up with him. 'Oh, he is short of brass, he wants a pint,' Billy said. Well, I got used to him but only after I had told him to try English next time. In response, he let out some awful exclamation towards me.

Now, in the trenches, Danny wanted to go and walk round a bit, he wanted to know a bit more than a seven feet deep, two and a half yard wide trench. So we trotted off, 'Tell Billy we would be no more than ten minutes for fear we were wanted.'

We turned left out of our position; it went round like a letter 'P'. When we got half way, it went up on to the top and down on the other side so, instead of going down back, we said 'Let's rush over into the other side.' We did and sank up to our puttees almost to the knees and the smell was vile. Looking back, we saw a black arm with its fingers sticking up. We scrambled up and threw sand on our puttees and boots which stank awfully. We knocked that arm down and threw sand in to stop the flies. We crept back to clean ourselves. The old 1st lads roared, 'That will larn thee.' Billy helped us to clean our boots. The sun was hot so our puttees dried quickly.

Things get serious

The War Diaries show that, 21st to 27th July, the Battalion were based on Gully Beach, leaving at 3pm on the 27th and moving up to the trenches, arriving at 6pm.

From 28th July until the 19th August, the four Companies spent time in the trenches, relieving each other as necessary. There were 6 days in this time, when the Battalion were able to re-equip, make good shortages, bathe and rest back at Gully Beach.

Amongst other movements, the men proceeded to Eski Lines trench via the Eastern Mule Track. They took over part of the firing line including Essex Knoll and Woster Flat.

I didn't take to my platoon Sergeant. It would be best not to name him.

I got orders to lead my section over the top, in the morning at 4.10am. Following in support of C Company, all our company was to be over in a line but I had orders to obey to the letter. To cut it short, we got the whistle call for us all to go up and over in rushes. We got shelled, machine-gunned, bombed, some wounded and some dropped.

Still, we went on, our C Company, on ahead. However, we got driven back and ordered to get back to our old position in Bond Street. Early next morning, one of our cooks crawled into our trench, wounded in the leg saying, 'Thousands of them in Krithia. Thousands of them.' We patched up his leg between the knee and the thigh.

I was hurt after that fight. Private Danny Hodson was carried back and died, his pal, Private Billy Hale, was wounded. I had two elderly soldiers with me that had trained at Hull with the 3rd Battalion Lancashire Fusiliers, Private Lew Knowles and Private Paddy Murphy.

Some nights, I tried to keep them off patrols if I thought the Turks were active with machine guns, we got used to their habits. When on patrol, we had to be quick and drop at the first blast, a shell hole was best. On trench duty, I gave them breakfast, dinner and tea and we tried to keep the trench clean.

We had a good spell in the line strengthening, improving and deepening a communication trench down to the beach. We didn't use sand bags, just earth, some clay and sand. Weeks went by without anything happening.

One night, I had a clash with my platoon Sergeant Mc ... I went out on patrol at midnight with two brothers. I won't say their names. Our Captain was a queer sort, always, at night, walking on the top in front of our line, just a yard in front. We got used to him but we wondered why he did it because if a sentry was asleep, he could tell down in the trench just as on top.

The Captain was waiting for me at the trench where our patrol went out, and which was opposite a gap in the wire. He got me to stand up on the fire step looking over the top and said, 'You see the big tree 50 or 60 yards towards the Turks, the only one near us. You will make straight for it and you will come first to our wire about 25 yards away where there is a gap. Go through it, turn right and after about 30 yards you will come to the next gap then go left through that gap. Then, it is left again to another gap, turn right and the last gap will lead you into no man's land. From there you will patrol, 100 yards each side of the last gap. You will be out till 1am. Keep down as much as possible, listen and look, be careful and don't make a sound. Give me a report when you get back.'

The word was sent along the line, both right and left, that a patrol was going out and there should be no firing. After we received the 'message received and understood', the two brothers and I went over and crept towards the wire.

We got to the wire but could not see the gap. One of the brothers got into a shell hole and his brother and I went on for 50 yards either side of the shell hole to look for the gap but it was hopeless. Near us was a broken cart shaft so we placed it between the wires and a post and quietly forced a gap big enough to go through. When we had the gap big enough to go through, I told them to get going.

However, the younger brother was still in the shell hole and wouldn't budge. I told him he would be court-martialled but he didn't care. 'Corporal, I promise I will stay until you both get back,' he said. His brother pleaded for him, 'It will be hard for me if he is branded. He has done it before. I will go and do anything you want but he hasn't the courage, Corporal.' I risked it; we got through the other lanes all right and carried on as we were told to. Everywhere was quiet; there were no shells, machine guns or bombs.

We could hear transport in the hills, but not a shot. When I thought 60 minutes had gone, half of it spent making a gap, we picked up 'junior' and I had to talk to him. 'I ought to put you on a charge.' 'Please Corporal, don't. I dare not talk about it so you will be all right.'

I forgot it when I made the report out. My report read, 'I, L/Cpl Gregson, with two Privates, patrolled 200 yards of our frontage at 24 hours (24:00) and found it very quiet, nothing happened, the stillness broken by the enemy. They had transport moving in the distance, we couldn't see them, only hear it. I couldn't find your gap so I made one big enough.' I signed the report and took it up to the Company HQ and was told to wait by the sentry.

Our Captain came out, walked back to the trench with me and said, 'I will go out with you, Corporal, but not your men.' Again, after the message was received that there would be no firing, we went out and up to the wire.

The Captain pointed at the gap and said, 'Who did that?'

'We did, Sir.'

'How did you do that without making a sound?' he then asked.

'With that as a lever,' I replied referring to the cart shaft that was still there. 'Yes, I had got through holding the top strand of that spiked wire.'

The Captain went and sat in the shell hole. 'In your report, you mentioned a gap wasn't in the wire where indicated. But, you don't mention the body of a dead Turk.'

'We didn't see any bodies live or dead, Turk or English, Sir.' I replied.

'Are you sure you didn't?' responded the Captain. 'Yes, Sir, the brothers will tell you the same if you ask.'

'No, I have a better plan. I will send Sergeant Mc ... and his two Privates again. An hour ago, he reported that it had been there.'

When we dropped back into the trench, he sent the duty Corporal to tell Sergeant Mc ... to bring his patrol and a stretcher bearer to the 'going out' trench. He told him he wanted the body buried as, 'it must be foul by now as we have had no battle or raids with the Turks for some time.' When the Sergeant and two Privates came, I was dismissed.

The Sergeant did go out and when he came back he said, 'It must have been taken in by the Turks, Sir, it has gone.' The Captain hesitated for a while, considering whether to go out with him and look for himself because if a body had been there so long, you would be able to tell if it had been removed just one hour ago.

I don't know how the Sergeant got on with the Captain but I know the Sergeant wasn't happy with me.

Next day our Sergeant said, 'Next time you go on patrol, you will come to see me first.'

'Why, Sergeant?' I asked.

'Because I say so! I can tell you how to go about it and I will put you all on a charge if you don't do as I tell you.' I guessed the Captain had given him a bad time. I assumed that the Sergeant was getting the grief for the confusion over the body in the shell hole.

I replied to the Sergeant, 'Our Captain had told me that I had done quite well and, if that's all there is to it, I wouldn't want any instructions.' I must have upset him as he went wild. 'I'll make a charge out, it's insubordination.'

'You do that, Sergeant. I'll be there when wanted.' War was toughening me up. We didn't hit it off so well after that.

We got relieved down to Gully Beach from the high cliff due out facing the Mediterranean Sea which was calm, clean, clear and warm. The sun was blazing, what more did we want! We had our first swim, we had stripped off but we would never take everything off so we were always ready if needed to go up to the line or up for support.

But when out at rest here, we could go 50 yards up to a marker buoy. If you went past, a whistle would be blown and a pilot motor would go out and bring you in and you were 'for orders.'

We had seven lovely nights and days. In the best of weather, every second morning, a Greek man in his boat would be tied up to some sharp rock with two planks stretching between the beach edge and his bow. He sold fruit and sweet chocolate, tinned fruit and fresh dates, figs and Turkish delight. You could only go up to him one at a time. He took your money first and then asked you what you wanted, he would offer you dates, figs or Turkish delight to make it up to your monies. He never gave change. You knew in the first place, he did not give change. You had two days to prepare for him. He went back in the dark and returned in the dark and was always ready at day-break.

It was home from home. When we got back after our relief, it was initially in support then in the front. In fact, we were more to the left front, one mile from the sea shore. Our trench sloped down that way.

We knew something like a landing was taking place in front on our extreme left. Shells, bombs and machine guns were all going off. The time was 4.30am and it lasted 24 hours, quietened and then started again. The landing was at Suvla Bay.

Off to Suvla Bay

After 48 hours, our 1st Battalion Lancashire Fusiliers had orders to go at once because the landing needed help. We were rushed down the slope to the beach when it was quite dark. We filled motor boats with 30 to 40 men in each. The marines were telling us that we were off to Suvla Bay where the new armies made a landing a few days ago. The sailors couldn't do enough for us giving us cigarettes and bottles full of water, all little things that meant a lot. They wished us, 'Good luck, chums.'

According to the Lancashire Fusiliers Annual, *'on 19th August at 10am, the Battalion embarked for Suvla. The 29th Division was to take part in a supreme effort to cut the enemy's communications.'*

The War Diary reported for the 19th August, *'Embarked at W Beach at 10:30pm. SS Clacton – disembarked by lighter at Suvla Bay – 4am on 20th.'*

We got out, jumped in the water then made our way across the beach into a small trench parallel with the shore. When all was completed, we were told what to do, and when to rush forward.

The War Diary continues for the 20th and then the 21st August respectively: *(20th) Bivouaced close to landing – marched off to Chocolate Hill at 9am and rested in rear of the fort until daylight.*

(21st) Moved to Brigade Reserve at 10:30am and made necessary arrangements for attack on Hill 112 at 3:30pm. Bombardment commenced at 2:30pm. Battalion advanced by Coy, beginning with A Coy at 3:30pm as reinforcements to the Munsters: B, C & D Coys at intervals of 40 minutes. Fire broke out on the ground over which we had to advance & rather disorganised things. Casualties – NCO's and Men 222 – Killed 17, Wounded 50, Missing 155. Officers 12 wounded.

By platoon, we rushed 50 yards down, waited and then repeated. With only slight losses, we reached some hurriedly dug trenches. At night, we moved up through a communication trench which was still being finished.

We got in support of the Munsters and the Dublins, who had to go over early morning on the Saturday 21st August. We passed the time improving trenches. The guns roared from 3am till 4am. The bombs and machine guns could be heard. We crept up and up by the bushes which were well known to us now.

Mid-day, with the sun blazing overhead and our A Company, following up the advance in rushes, had all reached a hill top. Our No. 1 platoon B Company went over. Our platoon was told to halt half way up that hill. We had to keep down; I was with my section on the extreme right. The hill sloped down to the sea four miles away. The land got flat before it reached the water.

I could see our new troops advancing under shell fire, some bursting right in the middle of the platoons. The Turks had brought up strong reinforcements when our officers called a halt because they thought fresh water and food would be best for the units taking part in the landing. It was a mistake, twelve hours of hardship would have been better than trying all over again like now.

The Turks knew we would come. That landing had taken them by surprise but not now. Our division was to keep the Turks away from Suvla Bay.

The Lancashire Fusiliers Annual reported: *'on the 21st August, the*

29th Division was to attack the south-west corner of the Anafarta Sagir Spur, part of the Anafarta Ridge. Sir Ian Hamilton said, 'this spur forms a strong natural barrier. It rises 350ft from the plain with steep spurs jutting out to the west and south-west, the whole of it covered with dense holly-oak scrub, so nearly impenetrable that it breaks up an attack and forces troops to move in single file along goat tracks.'

But few guns had been landed, and the chief dependence for this arm was the Battleships. The 29th Division was to attack a line running from Hill 70 (also known as Scimitar Hill) to Chocolate Hill (also known as Hill 112). Precisely at 3pm, the attack was opened from both hills. The 1st Battalion under Lieutenant-Colonel Pearson was at Chocolate Hill.

The enemy's shell-fire was so severe that the gorse was set on fire and the Battalion was forced to leave its position amid a furious fire, and consequent explosions of ammunition. The machine gun and rifle fire swept the whole position and the casualties were heavy.

At 4:12pm, Lieutenant-Colonel Pearson received a report from the Officer Commanding the Munster Fusiliers that his Battalion was held up owing to loss of officers. Colonel Pearson ordered A Company to advance and support them, a few minutes later B Company was ordered to reinforce A Company. Somewhat later, C Company was sent out to pick up the line of A and B Companies. The Munsters were about 500 feet in front of the Lancashire Fusiliers' line.

Colonel Pearson sent out a message to the Brigadier with a suggestion that the Royal Fusiliers should support the Lancashire and Munster Fusiliers. At 5:30pm, the officer commanding A company sent out a report that he was supporting the Munsters but he was wounded. Within an hour, the senior NCO of A Company sent in word that only four men remained unwounded. Most of the casualties occurred in the first 50 yards of the advance. At 6:20pm, there was a renewed burst of fire from Chocolate Hill (Hill 112). A few minutes later, the Sergeant-Major of the Munsters reported to Colonel Pearson that there were 150 men unwounded at the entrance to the trench. Captain Geddes was to send them forward but they subsequently retired to a trench occupied by the Dublin Fusiliers.

At about 7:30pm, there was no one alive in front of the trench occupied by the Lancashire Fusiliers and the Dublin Fusiliers.

Next morning 22nd August, the 1st Battalion could only muster 13 officers and 315 NCO's and men.

At 4pm, the Battalion returned to Chocolate Hill but on the following day was in reserve, the firing line being held by the Royal Fusiliers, Royal Munsters and Royal Dublin Fusiliers.

It had been a costly landing. Our platoon officer, Lieutenant G. G. Needham, was hit and killed in that attack, on that hill, after he gave us orders to go over.

He was from Werneth, near Oldham, and had gone to Hulme Grammar School in Oldham. We used to talk together, when we clashed on night duty hours, about England. He was interested in our training before going out.

He knew Colonel Turner Commanding Officer (4th Battalion Lancashire Fusiliers) and Captain Madeley, Adjutant Sergeant. Sergeant Eccles was with him at Nuneaton where the 1st Battalion was stationed on commencement of the war. What I did and where and my running was a big topic of conversation between us. He was a good officer, a bonny man, clean, reddish tan, plump face, fearless, good natured and spoke quietly. He was Mentioned in Despatches and is Remembered with Honour at Hill 10 Cemetery.

Back in our trench, an officer gave us orders to get to within four yards, take off our equipment and put our rifles down.

At the whistle, we were to go over and make sure we brought back a wounded comrade. 'No Dead' were to be brought back, though.

When that whistle was blown, I darted up, threw myself over that ridge and rolled down. I looked about and saw a youth down on his side holding his knee. I bandaged it tight and lifted him. He couldn't walk and fell. I moistened his lips, lifted him, struggled up, then got him on my back, my arm around his neck and heaved up and over.

He was hit again in his side around the hip. I put him down and plugged the hole as best I could. The hole, you could have put a penny into it.

He was in pain. I carried him, struggled, put him down, picked him up and got him into that trench that we had improved. A wounded Irishman had seen this and he helped me along the trench to the first aid post.

The Sergeant took us in to a dug out. We put the youth down on the earth table. A short time after, the Doctor came out. He said, 'Corporal, you have done your best. Stopping the blood was the best thing you could have done. It could be you have saved his life.' I tell you now, it didn't.

I got up that mount and put on my things and got my rifle. There were only a few rifles.

On that hillside later, a section gathered the injured up and brought them into our trench. We had seven missing when Lieutenant called the roll. We rested that night.

Next day, the job was to dig and make the line fit for live soldiers to live in. The 29th Division style was to line the trench with a wall of sand bags, they didn't trust just earth. It was sandy and gave way when a blast came near. It saved time and labour and it was cleaner for us to live with. It was just a routine for us.

The Engineers were out at nights putting up the wire which always reminded me of Warrington's Rylands Wire Works.

Time went on with nothing much happening. We got visited on occasions by a plane or two with a German mark but, rumour had it, he was a Turkish Ace. I know one afternoon he got cheers and flew round our lines, everybody firing rifles and machine guns at him and we saw him get up and away.

We were by now in Brigade Reserve away from Chocolate Hill and to the left of Salt Lake.

The flies were awful. We tried to get rid of them with disinfectant but nothing worked. I had been making Indian gappaties, as we called them. I had Lew Knowles, Paddy Murphy and Eddy Hills with me, all good chaps. Paddy was a time-served soldier.

Eddy was a good scholar. We had made a grater of a biscuit tin lid by putting holes in it with a nail and our entrench handle. The sharp edges were used for scraping our hard biscuits which became a meal. We scrounged bacon dip or beef dripping off the cooks. Making fat or dip with the meal, we used to put in currants and raisins and we begged jam. It was put in tins in the niches in trenches. I was sick of it.

My favourite food was shredded bully mixed. The four of us used to take our share of the paste and put our portions all together. We had a small twig fire on the trench floor; it blazed bright with no smoke. It took you all your time putting the fuel on. We boiled some fat and put our goodies in about four at a time, the size of a mince pie, no bigger.

When crispy and brown, we would take it out to cool. If you had any left, you put it on the fire.

The thing that agitated me was the old regulars came along and smelt them or were told our gappaties were ready and they wanted to eat them. But they would not go to the trouble of getting their finger tips cut by scraping with those sharp tin tips made by the nail.

I couldn't honestly eat those gappaties now. Perhaps they tasted so good at the time because our meals were always the same. For days, weeks and months, the food was the same. Bacon was regular when not engaged in fighting and we ate with a quarter-sized loaf, about the size of a brown Hovis.

The biscuits were a bit hard but you could have as many as you liked, tins of them were built into the trench wall. You were able to open any lid and help yourselves. Tins of bully were the same, you shouldn't go hungry.

Surprises, both pleasant and unpleasant. Dysentery becomes an enemy

Our Battalion got the surprise of ten day's real rest.

The Annual said, *'on 8th September, the Battalion marched to the beach and on the following day embarked for Imbros.'*

The War Diary detailed on 9th September, *'Relieved by Worcestershire Regt – last of Battalion left in the trenches at 1:30am to embark at Suvla Bay. No transport available – went into dug-out close by just before daylight. Were shelled during the day. Casualties very slight.*

At 10:30pm at Suvla Bay, embarked on lighters to SS Osmanich

It continued for the 10th, *'9am, disembarked half the Battalion on lighters – remainder disembarked at midday and arrived at camp at 2pm.*

We got back into those motor boats, 30 or so in each, and in the dark. We went over to the island of Imbros. It was lovely but nothing to get excited over. There were a couple of small farm houses, the few inhabitants would pass from the shore to their homes with their stores in a bundle on their heads. They never spoke to us. Up they went on a path about a yard wide, to and fro daily.

I was taken short one full moon night and went out of our bivouac with no covering. We used toilets surrounded with canvas sheets fastened to poles. I came out and walked round the back to see the background. It was almost like day, a bright moon and cloudless sky.

I saw a figure crumpled up on the field and when I rolled him over, it was a dead soldier. To be sure, I flicked his eye with my finger nail then ran to our battalion's sick aid post, where the Sergeant got a stretcher and asked me to help him. 'Yes, you are right. He has been dead sometime.'

Before we went, we had told the sentry to wake the doctor so he was ready for us. 'Yes, it was dysentery,' confirmed the doctor.

The War Diary reported on 13th September, *'Dysentery rather bad in the Battalion – 107 sent to hospitals. Battalion went on a picnic in the hills under Company Commanders.'*

It continued on the 15th, *'2pm, moved to new camp in the hills – the ground of the old camp rather unsanitary.'*

Another incident happened when I was on duty as Orderly Corporal for the day.

At 9am, I took the sick over to the doctor about 100 yards away across a field. The doctor called me in, 'You have a Private S…t (I am not going to name him) in your party. What sort of a soldier is he? What I know of him isn't much but he is an old soldier in more ways than one?'

'Meaning what?' I asked.

The doctor explained, 'Not clever, slovenly, grumbles if ordered to do a task. That's my opinion of him. I want you to get a sample of his excreta.'

When I got back, I told the Sanitary Sergeant to provide a closet for the soldier.

I told the Sergeant that the doctor ordered a sample. I went over to the doctor with it. He took the tin and, after a time, he shouted me in to his place.

'Can you tell dysentery, Corporal?'

I replied, 'Blood, Sir. I would expect to see blood, Sir.'

The doctor said, 'Yes, but not sprinkled on it … through it all, not dotted like vinegar on chips!'

I was told to put him on a charge, company orders.

I cut half way back and came across a soldier under some bushes, he was moaning.

I looked at him. It was Private Harry Gardner who I had trained with at Barrow. I didn't know he had come out. His pay book was signed for by D Company. I was in B Company so I had never seen or heard of him over there.

I walked him back to the doctor. 'Now Sir, I can give you this Private's character. He was in my section in Barrow. He is quiet, well-mannered and never disobedient. His dad is a grammar school headmaster from Horwich.'

'You know him, Corporal?'

'With six months training and living in the same hut, Sir, one got to know each other.' The doctor got him away and to hospital. Private Gardner thanked me.

On the 21st September, the War Diary stated, *'4pm, embarked SS Ermine – C Coy in SS Redbreast. Left Imbros 5:30pm and arrived at Suvla Bay 6:30pm. Disembarked 9pm and arrived in Brigade Reserve at 10pm. Bivouacs'*

The Annual reports, *'on the 26th September, the Battalion was in the firing line again.'*

The War Diary for the 26th explains, *'worked as usual in morning. Uninterrupted by enemy aeroplane. At 7pm, moved about 1 and a 1/4 miles nearer the firing line into Brigade Support. B Coy on fatigue all night with 2nd Royal Fusiliers.'*

We got back in the front line on the left of that hill I told you about and we got some six week old papers out.

In one, The Guardian (not the Warrington Guardian) had a photo of that Saturday mid-day scene I saw, just as I saw it. The picture showed the troops going forward in rushes with the shells exploding amongst them. It must have been taken from that hillside that sloped down to that land. The photo read, 'Our troops advancing at Salt Lake.'

We did trench work repairs, improving, cleaning and various jobs. We became sentries, night and day, and undertook patrols.

We used to have some excitement caused by a Turk's big gun, from a position about three-quarters of a mile to our left front in the hills, which turned suddenly towards us. That gun would fire then our guns would answer back sending the earth up. Our ships had a go at it. We would say, 'That's put paid to that lot.' We wanted to see if it was out of action.

Then 'bang', it would fire again and our guns pounded it with shells. He always fired again. We think he was on a railway because fire sprang back into a tunnel, a distance inside that hill.

A sad incident

On duty one night, we were putting the sentries up, one hour on, two off, during the night from 'stand to' till 'stand down' as we called it. All the troops along the front in battle stood ready with bayonets fixed for 30 minutes till dusk. Then the sentry post took over. I had four posts to look after.

No.1 post was on the extreme right of our B Company. Twenty yards to the left, there was No. 2 post, then No. 3 post and then No. 4 post on the end.

No. 4 Private (I must not mention his name) was up first, his post was in a position, a little way out towards the enemy and with plenty of trees, 30–50 yards in front of our lines.

A sniper fired at 'Johnny No. 4 post.' He fired back at the flame that we all saw. I ran round and told him not to fire back. 'That's what he wants you to do, to draw your fire. Now don't do it again.'

It was his turn on sentry post again, for the last hour before daylight. When it was time, I started at No. 1 post, No. 2, No. 3 and then going round to take No. 4 off when 'crack' a shot from that sniper was heard. It got the youth in his forehead and killed him instantly. I saw him fall sideways.

We had had a long talk when I put him up on the post, he would be nineteen in the morning. In the last year, his parents had bought him a new bicycle. He worked at Bibby's Oil Mills, Liverpool. What a birthday!

On another night, I was in another spot of trouble. At 2am, a Brigadier came down to me at No. 4 post.

'Are you on duty?'

'Yes, who are you?' I challenged him which is what we had to do.

'Come, one of your sentries is asleep. No. 2 post.'

He led the way and sure enough I could see the soldier's head forward on the sandbags. As the officer turned I shouted his name, 'Rogers!' All our Battalion heard it. Rogers answered straight, 'Yes, Corporal.'

'The officer said you were asleep when he came along.'

'No, Sir, I wasn't.'

'Give me your rifle then?' But he couldn't, it had gone.

The Brigadier said, 'Get it Corporal. I put it round the corner to your left.'

I went and brought it. I was on the case at 9am with B Company orders, then onto headquarters. That was his second time. He went down to a camp for soldiers awaiting trials. We all felt sorry for his brother who was a Sergeant in C Company and he was decent for a regular soldier.

The Lancashire Fusiliers Annual observed, '*During October and November, there was the usual trench warfare without any incidents of special character.*'

We didn't try any advancement. Time went slowly. I got on a duty which we could have stuck with for the duration. We had to relieve the Munsters for fourteen days duty. I had to take my section on a well guard. It was a well or, better still, a water hole leading off our communication trench. We had to fill old petrol tins which had been burnt out first and cleaned. We worked in two shifts, night and day. During the days we filled the tins at the hole which was camouflaged and made a nice room to work in. All day, we were filling tins, carrying them along the trench to a recess big enough to hold 100 tins piled on top of each other and in four rows. The night duty men gave them to the units when they came. It was all written down on a list; A, B, C and D Companies, HQ, RAMC and Engineers. The list told us how many we were to give each unit and we were not to give anymore.

It was carrying them from the well that was the heaviest job, there were hundreds of them. We had plenty of water that flowed away all the while. Our clothes got twice washed! The sun dried them in time for us to put them on again.

We had the time to wash our undies and other clothes as well as washing and showering.

There was no sentry duty and we were not working all the time. The boys got a move on so they could get rid of all their tins and then do what they wanted to do or get down sleeping at night. We were sorry when our relief came to an end as we were so clean, cool and rested.

Autumn comes and goes, winter follows quickly and becomes our new enemy

All night we heard crickets chirping, it was going cool at nights but it was still October. It wasn't cold but it was not like it used to be when it was warm, both night and day.

There was nothing to break our rather dull life. We passed the time throwing biscuits on top of the back of our trench and we would wait for rats to dash along the back top. We sat on the fire step waiting. You won a penny every time you made one squeak with your bayonet.

On 31st October, the War Diary comments, *'Generally quiet, sniping less than usual. Weather showing signs of breaking – misty afternoon.'*

Interestingly, the War Diary from 1st November starts to make clear comment about the weather.

On the 7th November the War Diary makes its first mention of the cold, *'Very quiet night.*

Enemy Artillery very active during the day but not against subsection.

Weather fine & warm up to mid–day when wind changed to the North. Colder.'

November came and there was a change in the weather, overcoats were necessary at night. But it was still very quiet, even that big gun had got fed up.

I always said to the boys that the Turks don't want to fight, only to hold on to what they have held. If we fired, they would and it was like that.

The War Diary reports a sad incident on 22nd November, *'Very quiet night.*

Brigadier General & Brigade Major reconnoitred the ground in front of the trenches with a view to digging dummy trenches.

16:30, at the conclusion of the bombing instructions for officers held by the Sergeant Major of the 2nd Royal Fusiliers, while the bombs were being put away, one Mills bomb appears to have accidentally exploded. Three Officers of 1st Battalion Lancashire Fusiliers wounded, one later dying of the wound. Court of enquiry being held tomorrow to investigate.

Weather, strong NE wind, dull.'

We only had a slight dose of gas. I saw the German planes about twice in six months that was all, and they were not there to drop bombs either.

Late November came and one night at 6pm, it rained – believe it.

The Lancashire Fusiliers Annual reports it thus, *'On Friday 26th November 1915, the Peninsula was visited by a storm of rain, followed by heavy snow and a fall in temperature which proved for so many beyond the powers of their endurance.*

Lieutenant Cox, Quartermaster of the 1st Battalion, who was at Barrow, said,

'On Friday night, the 26th November, two terrific thunder storms came up from two different directions and broke just in our area, such rain I have never before witnessed in my life. It appeared as if the heavens simply opened and dropped an ocean on to us, it came so fast. It flooded the trenches right up to the men's waists, then flowed down the main trenches to the Headquarters, and flooded the dug-outs to the roof, as we lay on a very flat piece of country. The surrounding country was soon a foot and a half deep in mud and water, the trenches filled right up to the top, and the men had to get out of them and stand on the banks and chance being shot. The water rushed down all the trenches like a mill stream. All this took place in less than two hours. We were all right until the back trench gave way and drowned us out of Headquarters. We had no time to save any kit, so we had nothing only what we stood up in. The lightning was so vivid, it blinded you for a second or two. I had the misfortune to get too near to the edge of the trench, with the result that it gave way and pitched me head first to the bottom and it was 6ft deep, the rush of water carried me down the trench for about 20 yards, when I struck against a tree and hung on until I was able to crawl out like a drowned rat. I made my way as best I could to my ration dump which was filled with water, and managed to get a jar half full of rum. The CO Adjutant, Doctor and a few men sat round all night on some ammunition boxes, which were the only things that did not float away. The storm commenced about 6pm and lasted till nearly 10pm. It was bitterly cold and the next day it rained steadily on and off. We could not get our things and they could get nothing to us.'

The big drops splashed onto the sandy trench sending the sand up. It got worse with lightening, thunder, torrential rain, everything. It was windy and cold and the trench started to give way. I was still with Lew Knowles, Paddy Murphy and young Hills who used to count the biscuits, always! We put out at the back of the trench, spades, picks, bully beef, tins of biscuits and some well-filled sandbags which just gave way on the trench tops.

I had visions of getting out with water two feet deep flowing down to the sea on our left. The moon shone.

Our Sergeant said, 'We are for it, everybody for themselves.'

That remained with me for 48 hours after. We got out at night about 9pm, there was not a shot. The guns were quiet, it was dark. We started to dig and fill the sandbags we had and put them out on top which marked out our dug out. We got building two bags thick along the back and then built two sides but not at the front where the loose, sandy earth was easy.

It was all about keeping busy and warm but wet sleet came in and our old trench about six yards behind us was three parts filled with water and trench mud.

The War Diary records the day as such, *'Quiet night.*

14:00 CO's conference at Brigade HQ after which the Brigadier took the COs round the second line and also gave orders that by Sunday all officers should have visited the second line.

19:00 Very severe thunderstorm, with very strong gale, and torrents of rain.

20:00 All telephone communication was cut off, and all dug-outs flooded out.

21:00 Reported to Brigade HQ that all branches were flooded, water had come in as though it had been a tidal wave, that many men must have been drowned, and few had been able to save their rifles and equipment. The men were standing up to their knees in water, behind the parados of the trenches.

Orders were received for the dig in behind the parados and that the line had to be held at all costs.

Soon after midnight, telephone communication was established between Battalion and Brigade. Reports were sent to Brigade informing that the trenches were in bad condition, the cold being intense, and the heavy rain and cold wind continuing.

The Annual continues, *'On Saturday (27th) evening, it commenced to freeze and snow heavily.*

On Sunday morning, there was six inches of snow over the ground. Our clothing froze on us and we had no shelter, but Sunday evening we got the order to leave a company to hold the trenches and the remainder to go to some cover near the beach, then our trouble really commenced. We had lost about 20 drowned but all of us commenced to die, frozen to death. I started one company off and followed with another shortly after, but only arrived with about 50 men out of the 150 we started with. When we reached our destination, I made men light huge fires and got all the camp kettles going to make hot tea, and some jars of rum, bottles of brandy and a case of port arrived. I put half a jar of rum in each kettle of tea, and let the men drink as much as they wished.

About midnight, I got a party of men together and took two bottles of brandy, and went in search of any men who had fallen out, done up. We managed to get 23 into camp, and only two died out of this lot. They would have all died, frozen to death, if we had not brought them in. A party of men went out at daylight with an ambulance, and brought in 17 frozen to death. You can tell how cold it was when the ice was four inches thick next morning.

Colonel Pearson, three Captains, eight Lieutenants, a Sergeant-Major and twelve NCO's and 512 men were sent to hospital suffering from exposure.'

The War Diary records the 27th, 28th and 29th November thus, *'By daylight, the men who were capable of work had thrown up for themselves in most cases sufficient cover to protect themselves against shrapnel fire. The water had subsided in the trenches to an average of four feet.*

A few overcoats, rifles and a certain amount of ammunition were recovered. Great difficulty was experienced in bringing rations up for the men, but eventually bully beef, a few biscuits and a little rum issued.

The conditions during the day were trying, men were huddled together in shallow trenches, dug behind the parados during the night with any implements they could lay their hands on. Any who walked about stood a great risk of being shot, in fact during the day casualties were fairly heavy, from the snipers.

A great deal of shrapnel was fired during, chiefly at parties of men who were given permission to leave the trenches, all in various states of exhaustion, to go to the ambulances. Of these there is no doubt a great number failed to reach the ambulances, and died from exhaustion on the way.

A cold NE wind blew all day, with a little rain and sleet at intervals and it is feared that a great number of men died from exposure. Towards evening, the weather got worse, developing into a snow blizzard, with intense cold, and men were still struggling down to the ambulances in large quantities.

At 2am on the 28th, the blizzard continued all through the night and the condition of the men so deplorable that orders were received from the Brigadier to the effect that any man not yet fit to fire a rifle had to be sent to the ambulance.

At 4pm, orders were received from 86th Brigade for the Battalions to move to reserve nullah, but Dublin Castle was to be held, and that posts, new saps 1 & 2 in the vicinity of C.5.2 were to be held. The movement of troops to the reserve nullahs and a constant stream of men could be seen for hours.

It was very fortunate that during this period the blizzard became heavier, therefore hiding the movement of the troops from the enemy, consequently there was no shelling.

Bivouacs were provided & carts with cover on, tarpaulins, braziers, fuel & medical comforts were also issued. Clothing was also issued.

All through the day, large numbers of stretchers were continually going backwards and forwards carrying men suffering from exposure & frozen feet.

The weather during the day continued to remain very cold with a hard frost and bitter wind, but there was no snow

On the 29th, all through the day, a great number of officers & men who tried to stick it out were forced to go to hospital, the strength of the Battalion had fallen very low.

During the day, the men who were left with Battalion were all entirely re-clothed and it is hoped a large number will recover from this very severe experience.

Brigade was augmented by 88th Brigade, an order to allow them to hold the front line and two posts in the rear line.'

It got cold, freezing, our breath was like steam when we blew out. The Turks must have been like us as they never fired. I had gone right and left early on, shouting to dig fresh dug outs or some sort of hide outs. Two men hadn't a shovel at all. I went back and got two shovels and a pick and told them to go for biscuits and bully but not to touch their iron rations until ordered to.

'Don't waste a drop of water.'

At daylight, it froze icicles everywhere.

Our platoon Lieutenant who was from Rochdale came just as day was breaking shouting, 'Corporal Gregson, where are you?' I bobbed up and got out.

We had finished and had our ground sheets over the sandbag tops with four or five bags holding the sheets down, sloping down a bit so water kept rolling off to the back. The hilly ground sloped to the sea so we didn't get the flow in our hole, it ran away. The old trench got the water before it reached ours.

It had stopped when Lieutenant 'Rochdale' shouted he was on the front of the old trench and sopping wet and cold. He was in a bad way. I looked for a safe spot to help him. I got to an old buttress which had given way with only a gap of a good yard to jump. He got across. I got him down our trench then got his boots off, socks as well. He had dry ones in his pack. They dried him as best they could and made him comfortable.

We had a fire in an old petrol tin, our entrenching tool knocked the top out then knocked some holes and, in it, we put a candle or two. We had some candles that we bought off that Greek man with his boat that I told you about. The branches and twigs we gathered when we prepared for our departure out of our old trench were used for the fire.

We had been given a cup of water each to boil in our mess tins. We had chocolate cubes from parcels the boys had received so these came in handy. We shared it between five of us. Our Lieutenant felt sleepy so we moved in a bit for him to sit up in a corner and he got well away. Before he got down, he asked me to try again to see who was on our left. He didn't mention to our right. He must have been alone on the right flank when he got to our dug out.

I went while he slept. I got in touch with some of our B Company boys but, beyond that, no other unit at all. It was now 36 hours after the rain had first sent sand up. Frost was the enemy now, not Johnny Turk.

I walked all over the place and I tried to locate that water hole but everywhere I looked now looked different. The communication trench was like a wide brook, flooded, iced over, and the ground was frozen with shell holes like small skating rinks. I got back hungry so it had to be bully and hard biscuits with the lads.

The Lieutenant said I was wonderful to keep on like I do. It was because I didn't want to be still and freeze. I found a night cap in the bottom of my pack and I gave it to the Lieutenant. He looked cold and our fire was dead. We had no more fuel and our candles had gone.

Our officer said, 'Gregson, let's go out a bit.' When we got out and away only a few yards, he said, 'In my position, Corporal, what would you do?'

'I would get going to HQ. What use are 20 or 30 of us? We are now at the mercy of the Turks?'

That settled it, 'Go and get all here' which I did.

Everywhere was quiet. We never bothered about the Turks and they weren't troubling us.

It took some time looking and shouting. It was light so I could see small dug out places, not washed out, and freshly dug. 28 all told, were what were left of our 40 strong platoon. Twelve were missing. Our officer had got back in the shelter to make notes.

When we were all together, we headed toward that old communications trench down a mile or two just to our HQ. It was now getting dark, freezing hard and the ground was slippery. We set off to walk four miles. Our officer said that it never seemed to end. We went a yard forward and half a yard back as we kept slipping back becoming weary, tired and sleepy but we kept them going.

However, the boys would sit down often at the rocky sides to the path. We had a steep walk up to a narrow, high bridge that we had to cross. We all stopped on the other side where there were several dead mules on the track on the other side of the bridge. There was no blood anywhere; it looked like exposure had killed those mules.

Our engineers had built that bridge so the troops would save miles and much time crossing the ravine. It was about halfway to our destination and it was about dusk. The path was about four yards wide and went through some hills which afforded us some shelter. It was now freezing hard and the bottoms of our overcoats were like boards. The sludge that had got on them was now hard. We had to almost force the men to keep going; they wanted to sleep both day and night and now another day had gone. It had been 40 hours without sleeping or a hot meal or a drink.

We finally reached our Headquarter Stores. I saw, and I knew he knew me, and called out to HQ Master Cox from the 4th Battalion Barrow. **Lieutenant Cox was quoted in the Fusiliers Annual as mentioned previously.**

'Our champion!' he said referring to the Garrison race back in Barrow. 'Give me your mess tin. He put in half full of rum and the cooks will fill it with hot water. Give everyone a mouthful!' which I did.

Our Lieutenant got to know where the Battalion had gone which was about a mile down to the beach. He was anxious to report in. He collected his men and made them walk on. It was hopeless, they were sleepless, tired and there was no good hot food or drinks. They just stopped on the paths. Our Lieutenant asked me to get some food. I went with two Privates back to the stores, half a mile or more. We got a sandbag each and filled it with bread, cheese, bully and butter. It was then a case of making them stay awake to eat, one or two did fall asleep.

Then the officers wanted blankets and asked me to get a volunteer party to go for them. My two companions, Lew and Paddy, said they would try so again we went back, all groggy. Sadly, young Hills was already down so I covered him with his overcoat and I went to the blanket store where we had to help ourselves. An old solider got us one roll of 12 blankets. We carried this out and then got another but it was too heavy for us so you can tell what state we were in; it was a nightmare. I gave four blankets each to Lew and Paddy to try and get just 300 yards or so.

We never made it. Lew, just in front, stumbled, went down by the road side and stopped there. I covered him. Then I tried with Paddy to go on. Tragically, Paddy did the same and gave out but I can't say whether I covered him or not as I don't know what happened next.

The War Diary for the 30th November states the *'weather improved a great deal during the day with a cold wind but warmer sun.'* But this came too late for me – the damage was done.

Going back home

I woke in broad daylight about mid-day in a bell tent in an Australian camp. I struggled out of bed which was actually a stretcher and realised that I was all bandaged up including my feet, head, ears and my face. I could only just see my hands bandaged and my feet looking like pillow slips, also heavy with bandages.

I opened the flap of the tent and saw down the ravine with huts on one side and stables on the other, Australians, ambulances, horses and mules. I also saw the sea and a hospital ship with a big red cross on its side. I stepped out of the tent and a voice from behind the tents shouted, 'Where do you think you're going?'

I said, 'To that boat.' He shouted, 'Get going you bastard' slapping his two mules which he had been putting harnesses on. They passed me and into the stable they trotted.

I stumbled down. I didn't think to enquire into how, when and where and who had looked after me. No, I saw that Red Cross and I didn't want it to start without me. It took ages and I was dizzy. It just happened that at the end of that valley in a kind of shelter, the Royal Army Medical Corps staff had hot carnation milk for all who called for it. I picked up a tin and got a hot drink. As said, it was an Australian camp and I made a mistake on not making any inquiries as to how I had got there.

I kept on going so as not to miss the ship. A thin line of Tommies were going out over the shore to motor boats. When I was spotted, two marines came running and took me by the arms and lifted me the remaining distance to their boat. We got to the ship.

I was taken to the theatre first. The ship's doctor said, 'Now, first, how did you come to get on board the hospital ship?' I started to tell him when he said that I should have been given a tab of clearance with all the particulars on from the doctor who attended to me. He was astounded though that I had made it that far. His staff took all my particulars.

I was taken to Lemnos and put into a big tent and given a warm bath by our regular nurses. They worked hard. They treated the wounded, those with dysentery and frost bite and, like I was found to have, those with rheumatic fever.

According to one of the nurses my frost bite was severe. She told me to be careful, 'Corporal, your toes are going dull. One is almost black.'

I got into bed which was small but it was a real single bed with no sand, grit or rock. I soon went off to sleep and got ten hours without waking. Upon waking, I got a bowl of hot soup with bread, nothing else.

It was about 3pm when I got a visit from an old 4th Battalion Lancashire Fusilier and Liverpudlian, Corporal Jack Heitman (John Frederick Heitman 5187). He had a bullet hit his heel before the flood. I remember him well from two previous occasions.

I was a Lance Corporal and was stood with a guard on the main gate at Barrow when Jack was awaiting two trials. Firstly, he refused to obey an order, the order was to keep goal for the Battalion football team! He always did keep goal until a Lieutenant Shepherd came and took Jack's position. However, on this day, Shepherd couldn't play and Jack was told to go in goal. He refused.

The second trial was for breaking out of camp and those were the reasons that I knew him!

Jack and I now talked about Barrow, home and Gallipoli. He had been drafted to the 9th Battalion Lancashire Fusiliers.

Jack and I started to reminisce fondly, particularly about one funny incident that occurred in the Guard Room at Barrow.

The time was almost 12 midnight and dark when we heard the main gate sentry make a challenge. 'Halt, who goes there?' The sentry repeated himself saying, 'Halt, halt, I say.'

We dashed along 20 yards or so and the officer who had been halted was told to advance and be recognised. The officer said, 'It's all right sentry, I am Best-Dunkley.'

'Yes, and I am best bloody sentry,' came the reply!

We, including the officer, all got back to the hut. He was time-served and had just come back from being stationed abroad at Tientsin, China. It was Lieutenant Bertram Best-Dunkley who rose from 2nd Lieutenant to Lieutenant-Colonel B. Best-Dunkley, V.C.

In the guard room, he pulled his notebook out to give me the number and name of the sentry on the post. I said, 'You cannot charge him for doing his duty, Sir. I am not putting him on a charge.'

'I want to remember this night he frightened me, a raw recruit with a loaded gun. Halt, halt slowly advance.'

I wondered if that young keen sentry on duty at Barrow that night ever remembered challenging a Victoria Cross soldier!

Best-Dunkley got the VC on the 31st July 1917 for gallantry and died in hospital in Belgium on August 5th 1917 whilst with the 2/5th King's Own Lancasters. He had been transferred from our 2nd Battalion Lancashire Fusiliers.

Jack and I talked of that night in the hospital at Lemnos, as we had both witnessed Best-Dunkley before he got the V.C. and it was an incident worth recalling.

When the nurses saw Jack, they asked me if I knew him. The nurses thought he was conceited and a 'know-it-all.' He had come into the hospital to look at the newcomers like me. He had been in eight days.

When first he spoke to me, I got on with him. He liked to leg pull and get his own way at Barrow. He was the Battalion butcher and good at it.

The days went on and the doctor was concerned. My rheumatic fever was worse and now one toe had no feeling in it. They were doing all they possibly could under trying circumstances, both night and day. One afternoon, I was being looked after by two sisters when Jack was seen coming.

'He's here!' one said referring to Jack. Jack proclaimed, 'The hospital boat is due in today and I think I am bound for it.' He promised me, and the nurses, chocolates from home. He was told to clear off, but not Jack, he got worse and the nurses clearly loved his mischief. At tea-time, one of the nurses said, 'I can't stick your friend.' I said 'He isn't as bad as he makes you believe. If you just took no notice and 'take it with a pinch of salt' is the saying, he wouldn't tease you. The more you get ruffled, the more he gloats.' The nurse replied, 'I will see soon if he is down for the ship which certainly is due in.'

The ship came at 6pm to be loaded and ready for 11pm next night. Jack came again, just to say goodbye to the nurses. Half a dozen of them chased him, they enjoyed it. For a change, he knew how far to go.

They were wonderful, there was nothing too much trouble for them but they were tired.

I got told that 5169 Lance Corporal G. A. Gregson was on that list and got a kiss from a nurse who said Jack wasn't on their list.

I was to be prepared to leave at 9am the next morning. The nurse wouldn't be on duty as she was to be relieved at 6am. 'I am glad it is for England,' she said 'first stop.' She knew that much but not the port we were heading to.

At 5am, all the nurses, the men and staff as well, got washing and dressing and doing everything that had to be done. They had 200 or more men to see to by 9am. We were given porridge, bacon and tomatoes, then six packets of cigarettes and a box of matches were put under the pillow of our stretchers.

It was time to go and Turk prisoners carried us down. I was picked up and when my turn came, half-way down that road to the boat, Jack came hobbling after shouting, 'Stop!'

I told them the best way I could, to put me down and they understood. Jack let fly, with some oath, that it was his turn to go but he was over-ruled.

I went under my pillow and took two packets of cigarettes. Having already given one Turk a packet, Jack snatched it and grabbed the other 'not bloody likely, Greg, giving Turks our rations.'

I told the Turks to get me to the boat. When they put me in line, they were used to it and knew what they were doing. Jack spotted another stretcher with someone he knew so he flew off.

I took the box of matches and the other four packets of cigarettes and told the Turks to have two each and share the matches.

They watched out for fear they got called back before they could get the cigarettes out of sight. They had grins all over their faces as I was taken onboard. Jack shouted, 'Goodbye Greg, I'll be seeing you soon.' They carried me into the sickbay, saluted, slightly bowing down, smiled and then took the stretcher for more wounded, I suppose. We got loaded and sailed at 11.30pm.

Jack was right about one thing. It was not to be last time that Jack and I came across each other.

I will now tell you it was Christmas Eve 1915 sailing out of the Greek Island, Lemnos, heading for Southampton and not stopping off anywhere else on the way.

We got fog-bound off the Isle of Wight and held up but on New Year's Day January 1st 1916, I was taken about six to ten miles to Netley Hospital, Southampton known then as Queen Victoria's.

It was a trip to remember even without a diary. I spent both Christmas and New Year on board ship.

In the afternoon of Christmas Day, I was carried into the Welsh section and looked after by the rich Welsh. We got plenty of chocolate, cigarettes and a bottle of stout or ale. In fact, at 11am everyday, the cigarettes came round.

PART FOUR

Rehab back in England January 1916

AT THE HOSPITAL AT Netley, I misbehaved myself. I could now get up and could make my own bed which we had to when we were able. We all made our beds and the sisters would come in to look and see what sort of a job you had made of it.

We had to fold the corners from the side putting them in the centre, turned under well. The nurses would then come round, undo it without saying anything and do it themselves. I got tired of it and told my pals on the left and right that I wouldn't do it again. They both told me to take no notice and be satisfied I was in hospital in England. However, I couldn't honestly take any more so I said, 'If you do that once more, sister, I will put the sheets on but never mind how you want them on. We have done it for a week and each morning you and others snatch it up and do it your way.' She remembered next morning, called me 'the lovely Corporal' and once again stripped off the sheets and did it again! That did it. I wouldn't do it again.

I was reported and put on jankers, picking up litter with a sharp nail on the end of a brush handle and putting the rubbish in a bag to burn. 'You will get moved on,' an old soldier told me. That didn't bother me.

I was almost two weeks in Netley. When I did eventually go, it was with three others in an ambulance to Dartford, Kent. I was fit to go to convalesce.

I got a telegram after ten days there. It came on a Monday. Dad had died on 19th January 1916 and his funeral was to be on Tuesday at 2.30pm at St. Mary's West Bank, Widnes.

This was verified by the police. My doctor was all against it but the army captain thought it wouldn't do me any harm if I took good care and did nothing rash. He got me clothes and away I went with the doctor in the ambulance saying, 'Straight back, no monkeying, you are not fit to travel.'

I was for home and that was what I wanted. All went off ok at the funeral and I got the first train back from Bank Quay Station, Warrington leaving at 4.30pm to London. I jumped on the tube and then back on the train and made my way to Dartford. It was 11.30pm when I arrived at Dartford Station and there was no kind of transport available so I walked it, got to my long hutment and flopped on the bed as I was, but not for long.

When I did wake, I was in bed. Two nurses and the doctor were putting cloths on my head, saying you will be 'all right Corporal, you will be all right.'

One male attendant told me that my convalescence was set back a month and I had just escaped pneumonia. I had to spend a fortnight in bed and not to get up at all.

That funeral was in February 1916. When I did get better, it was April and I was walking around the lanes into Dartford never dreaming that I would have a daughter, married with a husband and three lovely boys living there one day and, 50 years later, I with a wife visiting them.

I got fourteen days leave and then had to report to Hull, the Headquarters of the 3rd Battalion Lancashire Fusiliers.

The need to get out of Hull and back to Barrow

I had a twenty-four hour stay in Hull. I was going in and out of the hut I had been put in and one of my boots got splashed with reddish mud. It was caused by loose duck boards from the huts and it had rained heavily for a day or two.

The Sergeant preferred a charge. I tried to explain but was told, 'Shut up and don't answer back.'

I got company orders at 10am sharp and 'don't let me have to bring you.' I didn't like him a bit. He was doing his best to remain in England and was not afraid to bring soldiers up on a charge.

I was hardened by now, which had got me thrown out of Netley. I got to the orderly room just to be marched in, 'Cap off.' The Sergeant read out his charge. 'Coming on to the parade at 9am with boots that hadn't been cleaned.' When he had finished, the Captain who was a jovial sort, said, 'Your first day here and out of hospital, I read. Well, what have you to say in your defence?'

'Just one thing, Sir.'

'And what may that be Lance Corporal G. A. Gregson' using my full title, whilst he was smiling, which helped.

'Only that the Sergeant has charged me with not cleaning my boots to come on the 9am parade. One hour and 30 minutes ago, my boots shone as good, if not better, than his, Sir. If you look down you will see what happened. The loose duck boards getting out on parade did it.'

He looked, 'Do you always put a shine on like that?'

'Yes but when you have got them into that condition, Sir, it is easy for them to get dirty again.'

I hadn't cleaned the mud off, he looked and he understood. He said, 'Sergeant, you worded your charge wrong. Now, what to do is the thing.'

I was cheeky now scoring off the bully.

'May I suggest, Sir, you send me to my old 4th Battalion Lancashire Fusiliers at Cavendish Park, Barrow.'

'I get the idea. I will rub the charge out and get rid of you. Come in one hour's time, all will be ready.' I came back and I was told to pick up rations by going to the Sergeant cook.

I got out of Hull by the first train that could take me away. 'You change,' the station-master said, 'at Leeds' and I had to hurry over to another platform for the Furness Line.

The Guard had seen me rushing, 'Where to soldier?' 'Barrow,' and he opened the door, I got in, slammed the door and away I went.

An elderly gent in the carriage on my right said, 'A near thing, Corporal.'

'Yes.'

On the other side, there were two ladies, aged 40 or so. The gent would be 40 to 50, all whiskered up but a nice person. The women wanted to know if I had just left hospital. 'Well, I have but two weeks ago.'

Well, that did it. 'Where have you been?' When, how, what? I said to the gent, 'It is my duty to ask the questions first.'

He said, 'Yes, you don't know who you are talking to.' He gave me a card selected from his wallet. Mr George Trenwith, Duddon View, Kirkby in Furness, Solicitor.

The ladies had relations in the forces, not anyone of their own but they convinced me that they weren't enemies. As if their northern accent didn't give them away. I was really trying to distract them from their concern for me. 'You do look poorly,' I was told.

We talked of my family. 'Only son I should say?' one lady said. I replied, 'No, one of six sons, five of us in the forces.' The gent was surprised, 'Your mother must be proud. What does your dad do, if I may ask?'

'He died about 2 months ago. I was in convalescence in Dartford at the time.'

'Are your brothers in the same regiment?' one asked. 'No, my elder brother Jim is in Canada. He joined up there in The Canadian Motor Transport. I am next in the Lancashire Fusiliers. Our Bert (Ted) he is with the Navy, the mine-sweepers. Ralph joined up with me in our lot, the Lancashire Fusiliers. He went to Salonika with the 12th Battalion. Robert was too young and so gave his wrong age. With being tall, he joined up in another town where they didn't know him. The last I heard he was on the H.M.S. Devonport.'

The gent was troubled. He was more interested in, 'When did you eat last?'

'8am.' I replied. He looked at his gold pocket watch and it was 4.30pm. At Carnforth, 'All change' was ordered.

We got out and he vanished. The women said, 'Good luck, Corporal.' I didn't see them again. I got into the refreshment rooms just in time to be put in a chair by a small table for two or three. The young girl put tea, a small milk and a meat pie down on the table. I was surprised at that. Bread, butter and jam, an evening paper, a book, a packet of chocolate and twenty cigarettes also appeared. I told the gent that he shouldn't have gone to so much trouble. 'I wanted to. I was uneasy,' he said.

He was kindness itself without going too far. There were just us two in that compartment this time. I asked him if he had anyone in the forces. 'Perhaps, I can't say yes or no.' I didn't press him. He continued, 'My son left home as he couldn't see eye to eye with his mother. That was three years ago in 1913. We haven't heard from him; we don't know anything at all. It worries me.' When I got out at Barrow, I promised him I would go over to see him and he wanted me to.'

I got to Cavendish Park and was told to go to C Company at Webb's Farm at the north end of Walney Island. When I was going across to the orderly room, Company Sergeant Major Fletcher, known as Ginger, met me with a laugh, 'Were you homesick then?' I got the orderly sergeant to show me my hut.

I got boards, bedding, a blanket, rifle and bayonet, all that I needed. I was polished, cleaned up my rifle and cleaned without a smear of oil. Ten minutes to go for dismiss.

I sloped away and walked towards Lieutenant Loseby who was acting as Captain. He said, 'Corporal Gregson, it is nice to have you with us. I am just going to dismiss the company,' which he did. Then he walked to his hut with me whilst asking me all kinds of questions.

I wasn't in Ginger Fletcher's favour. He gave me plenty of work to do until I told him he had gone a bit far. 'What do you mean?' he said.

'Ask Lieutenant Loseby.' I replied. Ginger knew I was not strong enough for the duties he was giving me. I had been excused such tasks until I was medically fit again as instructed by the Battalion doctor.

Ginger walked off grinning. I didn't mind but I wasn't being pushed around by him.

I was detailed for pillar box coast patrol. There needed to be an NCO and two Privates for two hours – one going and one coming back.

We had to keep a look out for submarines or strange boats and, indeed, movement of any kind out at sea. We patrolled up to the extreme north end, put a letter in the postal box fastened on a pole then returned and reported to the guard room.

We went out at 11pm till 1 am and we were excused morning parade. The weather was at its best just then.

One afternoon around 4pm just after we had been dismissed, I met up with Corporal Webb. He was 6ft 2 inches tall but he had been hit by a bullet in his shoulder and it had made him stoop a bit. He also had a stammer and he was waiting a medical board.

He said, 'Let's put our things away and have a half an hour on the sand hills.'

We walked up the lane at the back of the huts. Company Sergeant Major Fletcher was coming towards us. He pulled up saying to Corporal Webb, 'They call you Tommy, don't they?'

'No, Sir, do they buggery call me Tommy.'

Fletcher replied, 'Well, do you know what they call me? It's the Ginger bastard' and off he swanked grinning.

Corporal Webb said, 'And he is bloody well right, Greg.' It sounded funny to me, just pure swank. 'Ginger bastard' and he liked it.

Yearning to run again but that meant being sent to France

I was told one night by a soldier, coming into the hut, that had been out on pass, that they are talking in Barrow that the Garrison is going to organise a race with four places to count.

I went out running the next afternoon, up around the shore of Walney Island. From then on, each day and on the quiet, when I was detailed for that patrol to the postal box, I put my running clothes on under my uniform.

When we got to the hut in the sand hills, I stripped off and told them to look at the sea for movement and I would run with the letter. I posted it and then kept on going round the other side. I then returned, put on my uniform again and wait the time out.

Corporal Webb said to me, 'You are not an old soldier, Greg. When you told Ginger that you were going to have a go at that race again, I worried as I don't think you are strong enough yet.'

Lieutenant Loseby asked me if I would be going for it again. 'Yes, Sir, it's in the blood.' He promised to enter me.

I ran in the race as an individual and not part of a team. This time, a Lieutenant from A Company based at Biggar Bank was first with 50 yards between him and me with a Captain of the Engineers coming in third.

I had got into something like a decent condition but I wasn't strong enough to train hard and ten days was too short a time to get fit. I was also too heavy and I had a further 14lbs to get down to my fighting weight of 9st 4lbs. It had been all the lying around in hospital beds that had done it.

However, all this meant was that I was booked for active service! Corporal Webb and others said, 'I told you, Corporal, you are sure for it.' I suppose they thought if he is well enough to run then he is well enough to fight.

It was 12 mid-day and Fletcher was at the dining room door with Private Brindle by his side. When I got to him, his cane pointed out at me. I was wanted. He said, 'You will take all your kit and report at HQ orderly room by 2.30pm.'

It was about a 30 minutes walk to the park over Walney Bridge.

I would see plenty of Private Brindle later in France and Flanders. It was just us two out of 180 or more men that were leaving C Company camp.

Lieutenant Loseby said, 'Don't be too hard on Ginger Fletcher. He had to pick the two best out of C Company and I told him he had selected the best.'

'That's all right, Sir, but a bit hard on us two who have been through it once and are now going again before some have had a go.'

Anyway, we got put in a hut with 40 or so men who were old timers, though not in age. They were men who had been out before.

We got everything we required issued to us. We also got a 48 hour leave home.

When I returned from Bank Quay station, Warrington, and got as far as Wigan, I looked through the door window. When we stopped, I shouted out loud. None other than Corporal Jack Heitman from Barrow and Gallipoli was there with three more men, a post Corporal and two privates. They all got in for the trip back to Barrow.

Out came Jack's 'bible' as he always called his pack of cards. The post Corporal said he never plays for money but that didn't suit us so, without him, we got started.

'All change, out everybody.' We had to waken the post Corporal who asked, 'Where are we?'

The porter said, 'It's Kendal. You should have changed. Well, you can't get to Barrow now until the morning at 7am on the first train.'

The station-master wanted to put us up for the night in a first class waiting room but we all said we would have a walk round first.

We went by the police station and the policeman on the door asked us where we were making for. When we told him Barrow, he invited us in offering to speak to the Sergeant. He told us to sit down and eyed us over, three Corporals and two Privates. He ordered five teas with sandwiches and said, 'I will put you up for the night. Now, give me your numbers, names and ranks, Corporals first.'

'Not me,' the posty said 'I am not absent.'

'You're not?'

'No, Sergeant.'

'Right, I am employed,' Jack said which surprised me. I gave the police Sergeant all the details, and so did the two privates.

He wrote a note to our Commanding Officer, sealed it and gave it to me to hand in the next day. We got wakened with bacon sandwiches and coffee. We shook hands and thanked him.

We had to appear at 2pm as per the Commanding Officer's special orders. The post Corporal called at Barrow and collected his mail like he does daily and we went with him into camp. Three of us, on the report of the police Sergeant, got away with one day's pay (one shilling) stopped and we continued to camp.

Jack got two day's pay of two shillings taken off him and he got two days 'confined to camp.' It seems Jack intended to stop in Barrow until midnight with some people he knew. Jack said he paid a Sergeant who was on duty to report him in as he knew how to get into the camp through the woods, then the cricket ground and then into his hut.

Jack did admit, 'I stole out of camp, Sir, and over slept this morning.' Two days and 2 shillings stopped but he avoided the Sergeant getting into trouble. That was Jack Heitman for you.

I would see even more of Jack in France and Flanders.

PART FIVE

France & Flanders May 1916

Hard to take but we're off again

Jack told me on our way up to the practice firing line where we were heading. We were in camp still in England when he said, out of reach of others' ears, 'Yes, it was Boulogne,' and this time we were heading for Folkestone. We spent a day in the camp up the hill at Boulogne then we were put into railway vans getting out at a goods depot, not a station. There were about 70 Officers and NCO's and Privates in total.

I had been assigned to the 10th Battalion Lancashire Fusiliers, 52nd Brigade, 17th (Northern) Division.

We marched to a farm and joined up to the ('old Tenth') the 10th Battalion of the Lancashire Fusiliers. If I can remember, I think the farm was at Boisdinghem. I was attached to B Company.

Jack Heitman was in D company and Private Brindle was in my No. 2 platoon in my No. 8 section.

It was mid-May 1916. **The Lancashire Fusiliers Annual for 1916 stated,** *'on 19th May 1916, the Battalion reached Boisdinghem in the St. Omer rest area, and whilst there the Battalion took part in Battalion, Brigade and Divisional training.*

In the middle of June, the Battalion was in Picardy and until the end of the month was engaged in working parties under the 20th Brigade.

On 23rd June 1916, the Battalion took over the whole of the trenches occupied by the 20th Brigade which was going to rest. For the rest of the week the British artillery carried out persistent bombardment of the German lines. The enemy retaliated and inflicted considerable casualties on the Battalion.

The War Diary of the 10th Battalion Lancashire Fusiliers recorded on the 23rd June 1916, at Bois des Tailles, *'that the Battalion took over 20th Brigade front from 2nd Gordons and 8th Devons.'*

The Commanding Officer was Lieutenant-Colonel Wade who was

elderly. Major Torrens would be in command if Lieutenant-Colonel Wade got promoted or wounded, which he did in the face. However, after two months with plasters was back again on duty.

The War Diary reported on 2nd September 1916 at Fonquevillers that, *'Lieutenant-Colonel Wade commanding the Battalion was wounded by shrapnel. Major G. L. Torrens DSO assumed command of the Battalion.'*

The Diary also records that on the *20th November at Ailly-sur-Somme, Lieutenant-Col Wade resumed command of the Battalion.*

I had been posted to B Company No. 2 platoon 8th section.

Do you know who the first soldier to meet me in France was?

Private Jack Hague, the collier. 'Well now, Sonny. I'll die happy.' I knew what was coming.

'Have you got a cigarette, Corporal?' 'Yes, a packet, Jack,' I replied. He knew I didn't smoke and was a source of cigarettes.

'Give us a kiss!' was a saying of his. I was glad to see him although it was in France. Yet, it was war and we didn't know what was round the corner.

So, all was familiar. As said, Jack Heitman was also there and got posted to D Company.

I had Private Jack Hague and Private Brindle, both from Barrow, in No. 8 section so we could talk of old times. We went through the Somme into Amiens and in the line beyond. Our objective was to hold on to some small holdings that our troops had taken.

We dug all night, filled bags, built the top front of the trench first throwing the earth out on top. The back could be built under cover of the high front. It was our orders, so it didn't matter much. We did as we were told.

D Company had to improve the communication trench up to our front trench. We had 8 days and, when we left, a week of digging had changed the battleground from unconnected small dug holes into one system. If you had wanted to go to your other section, you waited till darkness but, by the first night, we had made it better.

We got down to Meaulte for a rest. Then, on to Guillemont.

It was wet, low lying ground and we had to place duck boards down. We knew something was to take place. We were 'navvies' for at least 14 days and helped to dig pits to store shells. The big guns were coming up, some smaller ones going up ahead at night. The Gloucesters and others were going up and some coming down. It was hard graft. The weather got better, sunny and warm.

We got on the Somme front at Fricourt and Mametz, short of Pozieres, and went in the front line to hold on whilst our guns fired for five nights and days without stopping. If one battery had fired for so long, the next who had rested an hour or two and got more stones ready, would carry on and so on. Fresh gunners kept coming and going.

The Germans thought it was a bombardment for an advance at day-break. Then, before it could take place, Jerry would pound our front lines with shells and shrapnel at the time of day-break. That went on for, as I wrote, five nights and days. On the last night about 10pm, the Gordons moved in.

The War Diaries from 23rd to 28th June reported from the trenches, *'Gun and shell attacks and a practically continuous bombardment of the enemy by our artillery. Enemy replied by machine gun fire at night and an incessant shelling of our trenches.'*

And on the 28th itself, *'The Battalion relieved by 2nd Gordons, 2nd Borders and 9th Devon'*

I was relieved by a Sergeant from the Gordons who said they were going over in the morning. He and his platoon were being shelled. I wished him luck.

'Aye, we will need it. Corporal, good night.'

When our B Company got down and out of that long communication trench, we lined up and headed off. We met another company going in with two pipers playing and a Colour Sergeant with a flag staff. He was absolutely 'blotto' swaying from one side of the road to the other. Some capped officer rushed over and with the side of his horse pushed him into the sidewalk hedge. He didn't get up. We were passing at the time, but at my last glance, he was still down!

On the night of the Battle of the Somme on 1st July 1916, at 10pm, our B Company was relieved. We were the first of the four companies and we were due to march to Morlancourt on 2nd July. The communication trench didn't allow a Battalion to go in together. Going out, we went in single file carrying all sorts such as machine guns and boxes of mills bombs.

We were wakened with both sides firing at the same time, shrapnel, shells, bombs from the air, mills, machine guns, the lot. It was around about 4.15am. We couldn't get off again. The big guns were blasting away.

I got up and went and looked in the gun pit, twenty yards along the main road, just down in the field.

Tall trees lined each side of this fine, straight road. The men of the Guards were working hard, some in just shorts, vests and pants, sweating, wiping themselves on towels. I held a cup of tea and handed it round. Their Lieutenant Officer asked me to help and after a while they stopped.

Then one of the enemy opened up. I was fascinated so much so that I almost missed my bacon and tomato breakfast.

The Guards had the headquarters over the road. The Lancashires, us, on the other.

About lunchtime, the Guards' Band played by their Officers' mess. I went over and sat down on the bank by those tall trees listening to If you were the Only Girl, Pink Lady, Blighty, and Just a Song at Twilight.

Bang! A shell dropped just behind that camp, 50 yards away. 'Who's Your Lady Friend' was going on. It was marvellous, no one bothered to move. The band played on.

Another thing of interest was the prisoners. They came in batches, some wounded but still carrying the badly wounded ones on stretchers. The men were helping the German prisoners, English, Jocks, everyone that afternoon. Ambulances were coming back and to.

A big, wired concentration camp 800 yards down that road had been built for those Jerries. The war, as regards fighting, was over for them. On banged the guns as the Sergeant told me they had to go up two miles.

In fact, their motors were loading shells ready to go clearing everything.

It was getting dusk when a German plane came down and dropped more bombs on a very big railhead. It was a mile away at Montauban. There were big flames that went very high. Our A Company had to go and help. They were to release rail vans and push them back to safety. They had to save as much as possible.

A dangerous mission

A runner from our HQ came with a message saying, 'Lance Corporal Gregson is wanted at once by Captain Ormrod.'

Ormrod, 10th Lancashire Fusiliers Adjutant Captain, gave me a note with a diagram of a trench and an instruction.

My section, just ten of us, had to take spare parts and tins of water to cool machine guns and reach up to No. 4 section the machine gunners company. We had to pick the parts up first at the machine gunners headquarters in Guillemont and to see that the machine gunners got them. They were going over at day-break so we had a deadline.

He said, 'Corporal, you have been chosen by your Commanding Officer who said if anyone will get through, it's that 29th Division Corporal Gregson. So, it is up to you, Corporal. You will have to hurry as first thing in the morning they go over with the Manchesters.'

Our boys were not too pleased about being told to hurry up as, 'we should have been told an hour or two earlier.'

We got rations but no rifles. We were given two Mills each, one for each side pocket. I found the machine gunners HQ and their Captain told me which was the best and, he thought, safest route. It was very dark with the shell bursts lighting up our way on the main Contalmaison Road. The road up to Crucifix Corner was getting some shells aimed at any transport and reinforcements.

We had to avoid night planes dropping bombs on the road as well as the German's big guns aimed to hit reinforcements, transport, Alfy Gregson and the ten Privates in his charge!

It was tiring and slow. The fields were full of shell holes after eight days and nights of shelling, never ceasing.

At the crossroads at the top, a Police red cap stopped us and wanted to know why the Lancashire Fusiliers were going out there. He hadn't been told to expect us.

He said, 'You have got a big job on there, Corporal. It's wicked at the top of this road for a mile or more. You can't keep on it, spare parts or not. Corporal, don't take unnecessary risks.'

It had seemed to take ages to get there. At times, we 'got in' to get away from the big lumps of shrapnel that were flying all over the place.

The Police Sergeant told us when to rush over the crossroad and to aim for the long trench to the front line.

He had said, 'You have two hours to do it in. If the old trench is in good condition, you could do it,' but he doubted it.

He told us to dash over to the trench after three bangs. He had got used to the gun fire in the trench. When we did dash on, there were two more red capped soldiers. We didn't stop to examine if they were officers or police but they were stretched out, dead. Two or three others were there also. There was a crucifix opposite the Sergeants' dug out.

The old trench had been blown to bits by guns and planes. Unfortunately, the old German wire had got into our tunics and pants and got fastened up in places. Pulling ourselves free, our clothes tore like ribbons. We had to risk it and go out on top. We had to walk round or we would go down into shell holes which were too tiring to climb out of.

I had two petrol tins of fresh water and I was also carrying the machine gun spares, chains and bullets and more. It was heavy enough. It was also a warm night with shells coming in heavily and our time running out.

When a flare got fired up, lighting all around, we could see our target was near. I asked the men to go all out to reach the newly dug trench.

The shells were coming fast, squealing. There was bursting machine guns and Mills bombs. They whine on for two or three minutes. Eventually, we got round to the place that we were looking for.

A Manchester soldier, wounded in his shoulder, was being seen to by another. I asked if the machine gunners had gone and was told that they, 'All went over. They are 200 yards across the field. They must have got a German trench.'

I got the men three yards apart and waited for a shell to come as I had timed the gap between the big ones.

I said, 'Nothing for it, lads, follow me. When I drop, you do the same.'

We had 200 yards of no man's land to traverse and it was terrible carrying the spare parts and the tins but we did it in three rushes. However, Private Brindle, who was picked by Company Sergeant Major 'Ginger' Fletcher with me at Webb's Farm Walney Island, had got a piece of shrapnel lodged in his jaw, hanging down inside. He groaned and clung to my tunic back. We had another 50 yards yet. I said, 'When I shout go, get as fast as you can and I'll come after you.'

I looked inside his mouth he was spitting. It was dribbling with blood but, thankfully, not a great deal.

When I got in the trench, one of my tins was emptying itself. Do you know who told me? A Brigadier. I believe I was talking to Brigadier-General Surtees. He asked what the Lancashire Fusiliers were doing here and I told him how we were detailed at 20:00 hours to find the machine gunners. He said, 'I saw you coming over, Corporal. Leave all the heavy stuff with me. One of your water tins is hopeless. Do you know?'

I was too busy seeing to it that Private Brindle got in the trench but, yes, one of my tins was full of holes.

The Brigadier promised that the parts and all we had safely brought would get into the proper quarter. But he told us that we must get Private Brindle first aid. I had asked if it was possible something could be done.

The Brigadier's Aide de Campe went off and hadn't gone far when he shouted for Brindle to be taken to that part for treatment. Brindle had to rinse, a pad with something on it was applied and then it was bandaged to keep his jaw still. It was something like that but it is hard to remember.

Our troops were ready for another advance. Orders were being shouted, shells were blasting, German planes dropping bombs and German machine guns going off before those lads got over. When they did, the Brigadier took all particulars of his men. Brindle's pay book was used for his home address and other details.

'Go now Corporal, you have done well up to now. I will see your Colonel Wade gets to know his Corporal delivered the goods. He went as far as to shake hands with us all. He told Brindle he had been brave and told him to stick to 'your Corporal.' We dashed back over the battlefield again, dodging as best we could. We got back to that trench again that led back to the corner with the crucifix. When I got back to the crossroad, a Sergeant red cap advised me to go across country and not near Contalmaison Road as it was a death trap. When we got to the first aid post, Brindle got taken in and time didn't matter. We were dog-tired and we got a hot milk drink off the orderlies at the post which was very welcome having had nothing since 6pm the night before. We had bully beef sandwiches with that drink. When the doctor came out, he said, 'You did a good job, Corporal on your friend.' I told him all about it and he was flabbergasted, 'You took a risk on that last lap. That was the time that most casualties occurred. Your companion will be on his way to Blighty in an hour. We're just waiting for the ambulance to return.'

When we got back, I reported to Captain Pegrum. He said, 'I have to let HQ know when you report in.' I was sent for to give them an account. They said I had done better than they had dared guess. It looked too late to expect anyone to find the taking off place, never mind deliver those parts.

I told the Colonel about the Brigadier seeing us from the back of the newly taken trench. 'He also said, 'I will see your Colonel Wade gets to know his Corporal delivered the goods.' I added.

It was dinner time and I gave it big licks, we all did. From then, 12 noon and the next day, we were excused from duty. We were to only go if the Battalion moved, which they didn't.

I got straight over to near the Guards at 1pm. The Officers had lunch with music again with the shells and bombs. As I said, nothing mattered, the music played on. Well, it was sunny and pleasant so it didn't matter.

The Arcadians, Maid of the Mountains, Tipperary, Love's own Sweet Song, Blaze Away, Over the Waves were all played. One didn't care what was flying around planes, shells etc. They were good players and it was the nicest of music. I couldn't wait for 7pm. Perhaps it might be my favourite Pink Lady which was such a soothing sweet tune. I am humming it now and living by the road listening to the Guards. Hundreds must have heard them at some point as they passed the Guards Camp.

In my mind, I was in Bank Park, Warrington listening to bands like Crosfields and the Black Dyke Band. I was dreaming of those Sunday afternoons with Charles McKean, two cousins Tom Pickford and Clifford Mercer and Fred Shadwell who got me in at the McKeans. One afternoon, an Australian band came to the Guards camp. They played a selection of songs where the trombone player made his instrument do everything but talk. He made it laugh and imitate cuckoos and donkeys. He was very good and they were happy days.

Our HQ got to know from a Captain machine gunner that we had got through with all his parts. I know he was in that trench because I saw him when I went back for Brindle's ammunition. Brindle had dropped it in the last 50 yards.

Two hours before we moved off, our HQ got the Brigadier's report.

Lieutenant-Colonel Wade, said, 'Gregson, you have made a friend, a Brigadier. He watched you all the while you got into the battleground. 200 yards of shell holes with shells bursting all over the place.' Well, now you know what happened by heart.

The Lancashire Fusiliers Annual describes the month of July 1916 as follows, *'On 3rd July, the Battalion, together with the rest of the Brigade, entered the conquered zone and occupied trenches between Fricourt and Shelter Wood.*

On the night of 4th July, C and D Companies under Captain G. W. Thacker and Captain H. M. Adcock captured Shelter Alley and Quadrangle Trench, although Captain Adcock was killed whilst jumping into a trench.

On the night of 7th July, together with the 9th Northumberland Fusiliers, the Battalion advanced northwards to attack Quadrangle Support Trench. The Germans were on alert and both Battalions were received with heavy machine gun and rifle fire and were driven back. The Lancashire Fusiliers were able to establish themselves in Pearl Alley and some small parties actually found their way into Contalmaison and destroyed several of the enemy's machine guns. A party under Lieutenant D. Gale and Company Sergeant Major Harris captured 23 German prisoners.

At 8am on 8th July, a second frontal attack was launched after a preliminary bombardment by our artillery – not only on German trenches! This attack failed and by this time, Quadrangle Trench contained a macedoine of Northumberland Fusiliers, Lancashire Fusiliers, West Ridings and Manchesters as well as portions of the Welsh Regiment and Worcesters who were attacking Contalmaison.

At about 5pm on the same day, the Brigade was withdrawn and the Battalion went into billets at Meaulte and then to rest at Villiers-sous-Ally.

The Battalion had the satisfaction of sharing in the capture of a large portion of the German trenches.

Getting up close to the Germans

Our Battalion had to go mopping captured trenches. The first was a fine, big one. The Germans had big, deep dug outs. They had twelve steps down and then you turned right or left to get in. Throwing Mills bombs was no use. A thick wall of earth protected them.

We started and the first trench had three Prussian Guards and six or more Germans, about 3 days dead.

They had to be lifted out and put on top of that big trench. It took six of us to get one body up and out of a six feet deep trench. A hoist would have been a lot better than mucking about with three day old dead bodies. I would have enjoyed it better if they had been five feet like our own English!

I had only helped with one when my platoon officer Lieutenant Bingham came to me. 'Corporal, take two Privates with you, I want to know exactly our position.' I said, 'We are well back, Sir.' 'I want to know exactly,' was the reply.

I got two Privates and made straight for a big gun pit and a Sergeant told us to jump in. He told me the Kents were 250 yards ahead. We moved on with the Sergeant telling us to be back in one hour for 'char time.'

The Kents were in support of the Manchesters (nicknamed the 'Dans') who would be 300 yards further on with the Guards in front of them. So, I made it that we would be at the least 800 yards from live Germans.

We got cheese sandwiches with a cup of strong tea off the artillery men.

The Sergeant was a Salford man, so we weren't far apart, here or at home. It was 'all in together', even in war. One had to make the best of it and do your best to help at all times. When we got back, the German trench we were working on was cleared and cleaned out.

It was a good safe one, weather-proofed with a sloped trenched floor each side of the dug out's entrance. If it rained, the slopes would take it away.

Made to last, they built communication trenches winding a bit like a wriggling worm. The Germans perhaps had civilian help through forced labour.

We did some spade work at the nights, quite near the front. Trenches were being repaired and improved and we helped with ration carrying parties.

We had five days in the line. Two raids took place, one by our B Company No. 2 Platoon, my platoon, and we had to take some Germans.

So just before day-break, we crawled out. When we had gone twenty yards or so, the platoon Lieutenant threw his Mills. Bang! We went running up to the trench, 40 of us. The Germans put up their hands. 'Komrad!' We took 20 soldiers at least and a dog came after them. Private 5171 Jack Hague put his belt around that dog and went back and fed him with hard broken biscuits then a drink. Our lads sparing a drop each for the dog.

Our Regimental Sergeant Major Newman, an ex-London police Sergeant, spoke a bit of German. The soldiers got searched for bombs, revolvers etc. More important was who they were, what age, service, how long in the front line, anything that could help us. We only had two casualties, slight ones.

Our Battalion decided to try a second raid with D Company, Jack Heitman's company. He was a full Corporal now.

They did it in the dark with bombs with two flares fired from their trench and they crawled out ready when the flares shot up. In went the bombs, we ran, jumped in with fixed bayonets and, same again, we took some prisoners and there were no casualties. The Germans were taken by surprise, we would blacken our faces so as not to be seen too early by the flares. A white face could be spotted twenty yards away by a sentry but he wouldn't be sure with a black face. That dog stayed with us. You will read more about the dog.

The Lancashire Fusiliers Annual recorded the rest of the year, *'On 1st August, the Battalion found itself in the neighbourhood of Montauban and during the night of the 5th was very heavily shelled but only had 6 casualties.*

On 10th August, the trenches across Delville Wood were taken over from the South Staffordshire Regiment. At this time the situation in the wood was very obscure although the position of the German trenches was definitely established.

On 20th August, the Battalion left the line and, after several days marching, took over trenches at Fonquevillers. After the Somme, this part of the front felt very peaceful.

The Battalion remained in the line until mid-September when the Division was withdrawn to rest in the neighbourhood of Cercy.

It was not until 2nd November that the Battalion found itself again on the Somme front, this time taking over the line east of Guedecourt. Casualties were few, but the conditions were very trying. The trenches were waterlogged and little or no cover existed. The mud in places varied from one foot to three or four feet deep. The Battalion came out of the line after a very strenuous fortnight, when Lieutenant-Colonel Wade rejoined. The Battalion then spent a month in Picardy near Amiens, and Christmas Day found once again in action on the Somme.

On Boxing Day, the Battalion trekked along the heavy mud from Guillemont by Ginchy Corner to the duck-board walks that led to the front line. The penalty for falling off a duck-board was a very cold plunge.

The front line comprised of a few connected shell holes with perhaps the addition of a bit of old German trench. In most cases, it was well over the knees in mud and water and sometimes even over the waist. The duck-boards only went as far as Battalion headquarters. From there, one had to take the telephone line (much to the annoyance of the Signallers) and wade across the 1,500 yards to the front line. The rain was more treacherous than the enemy for those few days. It rained by day and froze at night.

One man fell into a shell-hole full of mud. His comrades struggled for hours to release him but the enemy opened fire with their machine guns and drove them away. Nevertheless, some brave soldiers took out hot food and hot drink to the man and did their best to give him heart and courage until a more effective rescue could be made. After several hours, however, the man died. Many men escaped the same fate narrowly.

The Battalion had Christmas dinner about a month late. Major (now Lieutenant-Colonel) Torrens provided a luxurious spread to which the men did justice.

The end of January found the Battalion in the line a little south from where it had been at Christmas and New Year. The steady, dry, hard frost and snow had made conditions a little better. The line here was also rugged, at one point, only 20 yards separated a post from one of the enemies.

The Lancashire Fusiliers Annual continues, 'Towards the end of February 1917, the Battalion was withdrawn from 'scenes of labour' for a 'rest', which was actually, strenuous training.

There were many bright spots and many good times, however, and it was far from being 'all work and no play.' Perhaps one of the best afternoons was one in which all the Battalion turned out for a cross-country run. Sergeant Gregson won rather easily but quite a large number of men made good time for the distance.

During this training, Lieutenant-Colonel T. S. H. Wade rejoined the Battalion. Afterwards, the Battalion moved up towards the Arras region to take part in that Battle (9th April to 16th May 1917). There was, however, an additional period of training before finally reaching the fighting neighbourhood.'

Drummy the dog supports us all the way

I will say the dog did not favour anyone. I gave him bones at night when on night duty. I used to go down to the HQ and ask Sergeant Swash, from Liverpool, for leftovers. His cook saved things for him after hearing about our Regiment dog. We were asked what his breed and name was. He was a kind of bull dog. Jack Hague christened him Drummy and fed him with bones, scraps of meat and dinner scraps in a half petrol tin.

We had made two calls to get food. One call at the officers' dug outs, the other at HQ where the cooks would save scraps until we were called for.

Water was a problem and it was the worst to go long times without it. We had to have a shave and a lather brush wash with the same water. If rain came, we would put a ground sheet up onto pick handles and spades. The rain would drip into the middle and then two of us would go out of the dug out and tilt the sheet until a mess tin was full.

We tried to make sure Drummy got all he possibly needed.

Yet, he never thought anymore of one particular soldier than another. You will see later on that he was a dog on his own.

When we got down and out of that line, we tried to coax him too, 'Come on Drummy, we are going.'

He only wagged his ears and tail. He seemed to be saying 'No,' as he just blinked his eyes. I told Jack to fall in with a final, 'Come on, Drummy' from that miner who was feeling broken-hearted. We left the dog. We fell in and got into a right quick march.

The Lancashire's Annual describes this period thus, 'On the 9th April 1917, the Battalion marched through Arras towards the south-east. There had been some snow in the afternoon which became a lot heavier in the afternoon. The men had to take shelter in old houses and cellars. There was little sleep for anyone due to the cold and discomfort but the men held to the Battalion's motto, 'Keep Smiling.'

On the 11th April, the Battalion moved forward to take up a position nearer the enemy. The Battalion was side-tracked into a field awaiting instructions and spent 6 dreary hours as a cold, shivering mass of humanity, whose only protection from the wind and snow was battle kit.

Early in the morning of 12th April, the Battalion moved into trenches on Orange Hill. These trenches had been knocked about a bit by our own artillery before they came into our own hands, but they did provide shelter from the biting wind.

On the night of 13th April, the enemy shelled heavily all our system with gas shells. It went on for about 10-12 hours during which box respirators were worn almost continuously. Remarkably, there were no casualties, although 6 men were wounded by the shells. One soldier, sadly, had a Mills grenade in his pocket which was struck by a shell and exploded.

Overnight of the 22nd and 23rd April, the Battalion moved into Monchy. Whilst moving up, the men passed along a track upon which the enemy opened fire. 30 or 40 shells fell near the Battalion but casualties were light.

What a shambles Monchy presented! Everywhere were indications of a very severe struggle. Men and horses lay around, heroes unburied for whom no one seemed to care. It was impossible to get the bodies away by daylight and at night the enemy shelled all tracks leading to the spot. The cellars, too, were full of wounded, whom it was impossible to move.

Before our platoon reached the communication trench, to go out off to the front line, Drummy was with Lieutenant Bingham and the platoon and he was in the centre, leading us.

When motor transport was made available for us for the first time, 'We must be winning' was what we were thinking. When we climbed up and into the back of our transport, Jack just lifted Drummy up and in. As Drummy would do, he didn't stay with us. He went over to other soldiers, sat on a lidded box the width of the wagon and got off to sleep until we all woke at Doullens. This was a lovely small town with the river running along its length. The General HQ was there.

Captain Ormrod, our old Adjutant, was now a red cap. In his place as our new Adjutant, we had Captain Milne now.

We had seven day's rest with Turkish baths and change of clothing. My section definitely needed them after all the barbed wire and mud.

I also had time to have three good runs for the first time in France. It was nice to strip, run, get a Turkish bath, rub down with a big rough towel and dress all in the safety of camp.

We got paid out twice whilst there. I liked that river flowing swiftly and it was clean.

12th May 1917 'A sad day for the Battalion'

Those are the words of Captain Milne in the Lancashire Fusiliers Annual, *'After a few days of real rest in the neighbourhood of Doullens, the Battalion was again in action in the Arras district, this time on the north bank of the River Scarpe. Weather conditions had improved markedly but there were strenuous days in store.*

After some preliminary training and practice with the Battalion, in conjunction with the Brigade on our right, attacked on Greenland Hill from Cuba and Conrad trenches with a view to taking Charlie trench, then held by the enemy.

While the Battalion was assembling in the early hours of 12th May 1917, an enemy plane appeared and flying along the line, dropped lights. When the attack was launched at 6:30am, the enemy appeared in strong numbers in his trench and also put down a heavy barrage on the front line. Despite the fact that they were outnumbered, the Battalion fought on for nearly half an hour.

Too much praise cannot be given to the stretcher-bearers and other parties who went out in daylight searching for the wounded and caring nothing for enemy snipers who were very active. It was sadly reduced numbers who answered the roll call that evening although their numbers were increased by some men who crawled back during the night.

The 12th May was a sad day for the Battalion.

The War Diary records for 11th and 12th May state, *'The Battalion relieved 9th (S) Battalion West Riding Regt in trenches south-east of Gavrelle and the following morning attacked at 6:30am Charlie trench. A Company under Capt Barrow and part of B Company under Major Comyn succeeded* *in affecting an entrance but were driven out by strong hostile bombing parties. The Battalion suffered the following casualties: 13 Officers – 226 Other Ranks.'*

When we moved it was May 12th 1917 and we went to the north of the River Scarpe, in the line and from trenches called Cuba and Conrad and attacked Greenland Hill. We took a bashing.

My platoon Lieutenant Bingham with two others, Lieutenant Knight, Lieutenant Hastings and three NCO's and six Privates were killed, twelve killed and eighteen wounded on the 16th. The Germans were on our right.

Our A Company tried a break-through and my B Company with Captain Pegrum had to support them. We countered and back they got. We brought Lieutenant Pollard back but he died before our doctor could do anything. Lieutenant Shepherd didn't report in at roll call.

We had a long spell when I was told to hold our ground at all costs. It was vital to hold it.

The Annual states, *'on the morning of the 16th May 1917, the enemy attempted to break through on our right without success but with much loss. The Battalion was sent forth by Captain Pegrum to reinforce and support, and lost several more men doing so. During this fight, Lieutenant J. C. Shepherd had a very narrow escape. He was standing with Lieutenant Pollard and a Sergeant of the Company when a shell burst within a few yards, killing Lieutenant Pollard and the Sergeant but missing Lieutenant Shepherd altogether.*

Lieutenant Thomas Whittaker Pollard was the son of Sir George Pollard and Lady Pollard of 79 Albert Road, Southport and is remembered at the Arras Memorial.

All fronts were active. We could see flashes, shells, bombs and day time planes flying low. When a plane flew back, he was dropping bombs. We were only ten yards from that communication trench, we ran in and down it. The plane went past in a thrice and we got back. His bombs didn't quite hit our trench, we were lucky that time.

We had to march for two days, resting in bivouacs at night. Then, off again marching. On the second day, we fell out for dinner.

The cooks now did the cooking in the line of march. When we got over to the roadside and down to wait for the dixies of stew to come, Drummy came from the front, leading A Company. We, in B

Company, were next, and when Lieutenant-Colonel Wade gave the fall out, Drummy like a good soldier came to Jack for some dinner. He was followed by Lieutenant-Colonel Wade.

I was stroking him and Jack was collecting a drop of water. The Colonel said, 'Your dog, Corporal Gregson?'

'No, Sir, he is the Battalion's. Sir, he is a queer chap in or out of the line.'

'It was yesterday when I first saw him up with Major Torrens and I. He is good company, a rare soldier, a stray dog who only needs to turn a look at us and then charges and over the men go. What's his name again?'

'Well Jack Hague here, Sir, has christened him Drummy, Sir.'

'Why, Hague?'

"Well, Sir, he looks like one and it was the first thing I could think of.'

'How do you look after him?' he said to me whilst still on his horse.

I whispered, 'The scraps from officers' mess, yours as well, Sir. We don't neglect him. All the men have spared a drop of water. If he needs more, I will go down to the cooks and try, Sir.' I was very fond of him.

'Some other time I would like to know who brought him.' Well, you all know but Wade didn't.

Drummy would often go off to the front, 100 yards along down the road, waiting for the leaders.

Stop the war! Back to some running

Our Lieutenant-Colonel Wade and Major Torrens were with us when we got into hutments in a lovely village. There were hills and plenty of trees and, better still, no big gun firing or German shells reaching us. We could hear a rumble at times like distant thunder, a very far-away sound.

The Annual commented, *'June 1917 found the Battalion in sunnier parts, resting and preparing for the days ahead. The Brigade held another Sports Day and the Battalion succeeded in gaining quite a good share of the prizes. June was bathed richly in sunshine.'*

The War Diary recorded whilst in Humbercourt, *'On the afternoon of the 16th Brigade Sports were held in which the Battalion, with 7 firsts out of 21 events, took second place.*

Our Brigade was to hold a Brigade sports day in two days which was too late for anyone to prepare properly for it. At 6pm, the orders came out. So, the next day I got out and did three laps of a field. Some sharp runs of 200, 300 yards, maybe.

Our lad, Private Bowers won the 100, was 2nd in the 220 and I won the mile. Private Sammy Potter came 2nd in the three-mile. Also, we won the relay, Guard Mounting and came 2nd in the Tug of War. In all, our Lancashire Fusiliers got 2nd place in the points.

In our Brigade, were the West Kents, the Manchesters, the Borderers, the 10th Lancashire Fusiliers, the Engineers, the Royal Army Medical Corps, the Artillery etc. So, we did very well.

In our HQ, was a Lieutenant G. R. Fryer. He and his older brother were at Barrow with me and he told me he placed a bet on me to beat a certain winner. He didn't say what the bet was and I didn't ask him but I was glad that he had faith in me. His brother, Lieutenant E.H. Fryer was killed in action at Guillemont on 6th August 1916.

I won £4 or 100 Francs for winning, also a 1/4th share of £4 for winning the relay.

I ran 880 yards in the 1-mile relay as well. We won £1 each (there were almost 30 francs then to an English pound). A nice day and 125 francs won.

Sports were important in our Battalion

Our Battalion held four seven-mile runs with all who weren't sick, too old or on duty to run.

Now, it seems that Private Sammy Potter was the Battalion's cross-country champion in England and, out in France before I joined them, he had won all the Regimental races easily. It was now Sunday and on Monday, at 3pm, there was to be one of the seven-mile runs.

It was nice to see the villagers going to Church not that I was a regular attender. The bells were chiming and it was a nice change from the sound of guns.

The excitement was mounting as we had been paid out and advancements were available if you wanted. C Company almost to a man were behind Potter to win over seven miles.

Our old 4th Battalion Lancashire Fusiliers from Barrow, like the two Jacks, Ginger Moss and some of the other forty men who joined the 10th with me, snapped up bets. The best bets were available about 5.30pm Sunday night after tea. Our Regimental Sergeant Major Newman used to have Sam Potter for his batman when he was C Company Company Sergeant Major but Potter was now doing the same job for C Company's Captain Woods.

Charles Newman announced in the Sergeants' mess, there was 'no one to beat Potter tomorrow, gentleman.'

That did it. Jack Heitman (like myself, now a Sergeant) was alerted. I should have told you that, two weeks after the Contalmaison machine gun spare parts affair, I was made Sergeant acting (with the pay of a full Sergeant).

Well, Jack asked Captain Woods how much he fancied Potter. '100 francs, Heitman.'

'Right, I take Sergeant Gregson.' The monies were handed over to the Regimental Quartermaster Whitworth.

Company Sergeant Major Toms spoke to Jack and he put 50 francs on with Newman. He said, 'I'll have a run round to Gregson's billet, I want another 50 francs bet. I could do with it.'

Jack dashed up the village to me. 'Greg, the Regimental Sergeant Major is coming. He wants a bet on.'

He wasn't gone long when Newman arrived.

'Sergeant Gregson, they tell me you are a good runner.'

'Who are they, Sergeant Major?

'In the mess. I was wondering if you would have a bet.' I waited.

He said, 'Do you fancy yourself to win tomorrow?'

'I never go about saying I am a good runner and I don't have big bets.'
'Come on Corporal, not even 50 francs?'

'I bet you 50 that I beat Sammy Potter. We don't need to win the race to win the bet. One man to beat each other.'

'Yes it does sound different. Gregson, you're on.'

A soldier, old Tom Chadwick, held the bet saying, 'I won't be giving yours back, Sir, you have had it.'

'We will see.'

About 7pm, McToohey, a HQ messenger, came, 'Major Forwood would like a word with you Sergeant at 8pm outside the HQ mess.'

When I got there, Forwood walked me down the village a little and when we stopped, he said, 'Sergeant, in the mess before dinner we

Company Officers were discussing tomorrow's run. It turned out it's a betting race. One of our young Lieutenant's put his cheque book on the table saying, 'I bet one to beat Private S. Potter.' He got mobbed yet he didn't flinch at 100 francs. When Colonel Torrens said, 'Your man must be Sergeant Gregson.' He said 'Yes.' Colonel Torrens then said, 'Well, he won the one-mile nicely at the Brigade but didn't enter the three-mile like our Potter. What I want to know is can you run seven miles?'

I gave no answer. He prompted me.

'So, now you know why you are here Sergeant.'

'Your mess Lieutenant, Sir, must be Lieutenant Fryer. We were at Barrow when I won the Barrow Garrison seven miles.'

'Garrison!' he said 'well, now I must back Sergeant Gregson to win.'

'If I may say, Sir, bet me to beat who ever they are saying will win. Then, I am obliged to come in first. I don't know all the 10th Battalion Lancashire Fusiliers. Some have joined up like me. You know those like Potter came out from England with the old tenth.'

We parted. It was going to be a two soldier race.

Potter was a blond and I was dark but there was not a great deal between us as regards build.

The Race Begins!

There was a good turnout in a large parkland where flags led us to the big gates onto the main road. We runners were to turn left out of the park, keeping all flag signallers on our left up to the church in the next village. 'Your own Company Captain will be there to see you round him. Take a ticket from him and then return by the same way,' were the instructions.

It was Potter who made the running out of the gate. He was five yards or so ahead and looked strong enough and very keen. Apart from my dark hair (yes, I had some in those days!), we looked alike with white pants and red vests.

I said we had each other to beat so I got on and tried to go on to pass. He wanted to keep in front so I pressed on to make him go faster. I knew I could stick this faster pace for another four miles. We must have done three miles because we could see the village's church.

I rushed past him, took him off his guard and 20 yards ahead I took my ticket off our B Company Captain. He was Lieutenant Freer (not Fryer). Sammy shouted, 'Swanking, ain't you!' as I passed him on the way back from the turnaround and went over to the left. I increased the pace slowly. As I said, I was feeling I could stick it out, passing signallers. They were saying, 'Take it easy, Sergeant, you are winning easily.'

I was 100 yards in front at one point when I got to the park gates but they were closed! Police Sergeant Moody said, 'Keep straight on Gregson, down another 100 yards and then turn right into the village street.'

I passed Company Sergeant Major Toms and Regimental Quartermaster Whitworth who looked glum. Toms with his big heavy eyebrows and moustache was roaring like mad, 'Good old, Greg, good lad.'

I took the tape by 300 or more yards – the first man. It was all smiles for the 4th Battalion old boys such as Jack Hague the die happy miner from Ashton, Jack Heitman, Lieutenant Fryer, Major Forwood, myself and Lieutenant-Colonel Wade.

When I was given £4.00 (100 francs), Wade said, 'Sergeant, for such running you have shone for us but you have also won a barrel of beer for your boys of B Company.'

I was thrilled, something for the lads.

It was back to the War

Anyway, let's get on with the war. We were not living in luxury all our days. We got billeted in Arras and had our Minden Day celebrations. The Lancashire Fusiliers officers had theirs in some hotel that was still standing (well, some of it was still standing).

The War Diary recorded on 1st August 1917, *'Minden Day: The Battalion reached Lichfield Camp St. Nicholas in the early hours of the morning. The officers of the Battalion had a special Minden Day Dinner at the Officers Club Arras. The men were entertained at variety and cinema shows.'*

We, Sergeants, were in a large hut. The platoons were in huts with extra rations and beer, cigarettes and the day off to visit cafes and estaminets.

There was extra pay, singing of songs and dance. A good time was spent by all.

Drummy was not neglected. All gave to him, whether he liked it or not, bits of chocolate, snips of biscuits, bully and cheese. He couldn't go hungry or thirsty.

In town, we always had plenty of bread, we could buy a loaf or two and we would normally collect water also.

Drummy was the one that couldn't be spoilt, he didn't come or go for fuss. Whether it was food, drink or sleep, he would just be wagging his ears and tail, turn about and go off. He took it all for granted, he was just a soldier. 'Uniforms' was all he wanted, nobody specific.

The weather took a turn for the better and we hung about Arras for rest. After spells in different sectors, we took over the newly captured ground and trenches just beyond Bapaume.

In extended rushes, our B Company line had to get past the ruins of the place when shells were pounding into it and we had to drop into holes and take cover at every possible thing. Buildings, everything had been hit and blown up. Men and horses had been killed and it had been that way for at least twelve hours.

One didn't try to drag the dead away; the shells were destroying the place, intent on wiping it out. The shelling was awful.

Promoted to Sergeant and now running the canteen

When I was promoted to Sergeant, I had also been asked to run a canteen for the Battalion. I said it would be a pleasure to do so but I would like to sell at cost price. Our Regimental Quartermaster Whitworth was against it, 'We cannot run a canteen at a loss.' Our Colonel Torrens liked the idea if I could make it work.

I had started with 800 francs. The British Expeditionary Forces Canteen Sergeant helped me to begin.

He only gave me quick selling items such as biscuits, in boxes or cases, large packets of mixed spearmint tobacco and Mother Scribbans slab cake.

When the 800 francs was spent he gave me 5% discount so I got 40 francs back and let me spend it on chocolate.

Private Tom Chadwick, a confectioner in civilian life in Rochdale, and Private Bill Smith, a Salford Corporation worker helped me to look after the troops and our Colonel Torrens was pleased.

Now, after the race, I had been given my running prize and, after the boys had mobbed me, I trotted off to my billet. I went by our B Company 'Farm Barn' gate and straight across was a cafe, an estaminet. Two Frenchmen were pushing a barrel of beer into the farm. The barrel was my running prize and Captain Pegrum had a grin all over his face.

The barrel was in its position, stillaged and ready for 7pm. It was 4.30pm tea time, then.

Tom gave me two 50 franc notes with which to buy cigarettes and chocolate spearmint. I bought four boxes of Cadbury and Nestle chocolate bars for the tee-total men and spent my prize money and more.

7pm arrived and the barn was looking nice and clean with straw pushed back.

The boys were down on the straw, some sitting on farmyard machines making themselves comfortable with mess tins at the ready.

The Sergeant and Corporals were waiting on and enjoying it.

The men were singing songs, both chorus and solo. One Corporal sang 'Just a Song at Twilight' and it sounded lovely. The HQ staff had come in just in time to hear him. Glasses for the officers had been lent by the estaminet who supplied the beer. Our Captain Doctor Smith was first up and helped himself to cigars which had just the right smell. Lieutenant Fryer came over to ask me if he could have a packet of biscuits with some milk chocolate.

'Help yourselves, it's free tonight.' Major Forwood had also brought a bottle of whisky and soda to add to the event.

A very amusing incident occurred. One Corporal was 'blotto' and he would insist on wanting to sing. Major Thaker, shouted, 'Let the Corporal sing!' In chorus, from all who knew Corporal Randles, 'Well, you've asked for it".

He was drunk and had no voice or tune but slowly he sang 'Shine on Silvery Moon'. However, he didn't get that far before mess tin lids as well as potatoes and anything else that was available got thrown at him!

Lieutenant-Colonel Wade took a handkerchief to his eyes. We didn't know if he was really crying or he was crying with laughter just like

Doctor Smith. They saw the Corporal carried by half a section, face down and thrown into the hay. It was fun and the place was in uproar.

We had another little drink about 5pm, but it was dinner for HQ so they went, though not before the Lieutenant-Colonel had said they had enjoyed our hospitalities.

He walked over to Jack, patted Drummy, 'Has he had his pint?'

'He's TT, Sir, but not his trainer, I'm not!'

I liked the Lieutenant-Colonel. We sang 'For He's a Jolly Good Fellow' as he went out waving.

We finished at 9pm. As regards beer, if you wanted more, there was the estaminet over the way and two more in the village. It was a night to remember and it would take another book to relate all the songs and comic verses.

At 11pm, Jack Hague crept up to Tom's canteen and woke them up. 'Bill, get us a tin of tripe and a bottle of vinegar. Sorry, Drummy is hungry.'

It was now October 1917 and we got to Proven about five miles from Poperinge in Belgium which we marched through and down the main road towards Ypres. We were put into huts and it was a good job too. It was bitterly cold with rain, sleet and snow on that march to Elverdinghe.

Lieutenant-Colonel Wade told me to go to the brewery that we had passed in Poperinge or 'Pop' as we called it. I got a half limber and went. My transport driver with two mules was Sam Potter's brother Tom from Nelson in Lancashire.

I didn't know his name until he said, 'I lost a packet over our Sam. You were far too good for him. He is only an amateur, not a pro like you.' I was surprised although he did resemble Sam in build, looks and with fair hair. We chatted, he didn't bear any malice.

The lady at the 'Pop' brewery was very nice. 'Yes,' she said 'come in Sergeant and bring your driver as well.' She gave us coffee and homemade cake. She could speak English a sight better than us two Englishmen!

'How is your Major Thacker? I haven't seen him for a long time.'

'He was wounded,' I said, 'back five or six months ago.'

She gave us three apples each from her own trees and a parcel for the Major, 'if it isn't any trouble.'

When we had finished, our two barrels, covered by a sheet, were up on the limber all ready to go. She asked us to try and bring the empties back as soon as possible.

Tom and Bill had got everything in order with the help of driver Tommy Potter. 'Sergeant, let's have the first pint.'

I said, 'Not now, Tom, it would be cloudy and not fit but I will see you have the first at my expense.'

'That's a promise, Sergeant.' Tommy said in a real Lancashire twang.

'Tom, come in the back door fifteen minutes early and bring your mess tin.'

6.30pm was opening time and a queue formed for pints. We only had a pint pot to measure with, and it was a good job as it made it go round to all waiting.

The Engineers and the Medical Corps were nearby and had got to know about the beer so they were pleased we could serve them – not all canteens did supply outsiders. They got called in next.

In the afternoon, we returned back with the two empty barrels. The woman at the brewery was surprised, 'So soon, Sergeant? Your unit,' she said, 'are thirsty boys.'

I told her Major Thacker thanked her for the apples. The Major had said if possible he would call and see her.

At the brewery, I saw a photo hanging up of a smart airman. I got up and went over to see it.

She said, 'Maurice, my husband got killed, shot down twelve months ago now.' She owned and ran that brewery. She was pleased that we had brought the barrels back.

She said they tried to find the barrels at the camps but some have been hit by shells and were left out in the fields. They couldn't get the material to make or repair the barrels and it would be better if the barrels were returned. She continued, 'I can't keep turning a brew out to fill ten or twenty barrels then the next day the same and so on. We want the barrels to brew again.'

I got back late because I had to buy in at Proven where the British Expeditionary Forces canteen was placed. We had to go in the front line from Elverdinghe.

There were two pill boxes, cement affairs, with shell holes which were half-full of water. Our first job was to dig so we could connect shell holes to make new trenches.

It was quiet on our sector but about three to four miles over on our right Ypres was getting all sorts of shells. It was in flames.

My section got to a hole that was too deep and wide to make it into a trench. We made the trench in front of the hole, sloping down to the back. The new trench would be drier.

Anyway, before we got relieved, we had connections and a communications trench to come down back to the huts.

I saw to it that there was more cake, chocolate, cigarettes and beer. I asked for three barrels if Madame could spare them, which she did.

We got rid of the beer but I couldn't take the barrels back as we had another spell up in the same sector.

When we did move, it was back almost to where we had come from, near St. Omer. It was early November 1917.

It was here Lieutenant Young (his dad was Rymer Young who owned the chemist on Sankey Street, Warrington) got killed. He was our bombing officer and he was demonstrating how to fire a bomb called The Newton Pippin when one exploded prematurely killing the Lieutenant and wounding two Privates.

We lost the Catholic Priest Father Berkely.

The Annual records, *'So, Christmas Day 1917 found the Battalion close to where it was on Christmas Day 1916. It was a Christmas of snow and keen frost and even on the front line, it was enjoyed. There was sad news for all ranks when the Rev O.T. Berkely left the Battalion in November 1917. He was merry and bright and his sound advice was relied upon.'*

Father Waters arrived in his place, a young Irishman who soon got busy. Coming up to me he said, 'Colonel Torrens recommended Sergeant Gregson to help me. I want to go and bury some dead.'

Early morning, we reached a first aid post. He looked at some labelled dead. We sorted out the Catholics and we buried them in a separate part of the field. I said, 'How about our lads, C of E, Methodist etc.?' 'Their minister will bury them' was the reply.

When we got back, he asked me in his tent. 'Have a whisky while I make you a cigarette.' I refused both, to his surprise. He didn't miss out with the tobacco hanging out of his handmade cigarette.

I was asked a short time after to go with Lieutenant Fryer to look for his brother's grave at another burial ground. He heard his brother could be buried there as he had got killed nearby. We searched but had no luck. I knew him as we had both trained at Barrow. We had two sets of brothers at Barrow, Fryer and Ravenscroft.

We looked at every wooden cross but we did not see a 'Fryer' at all. It got dark when we got back to St Omer.

We moved by motor transport to the Arras area of St. Catherine. Drummy was with us again. The weather was now vile. The rain, sleet and cold not letting up for 48 hours. Going up to the front line, we were slipping and sliding, clutching to stay on our feet. It was a lot better when we got in as duck-boards were down.

It was quiet. Their chemical works were nearby. We had made an attack on it the last time we were here.

Holding on was our job now. Not to give in if the Germans attacked, which they didn't.

The weather was too bad for rushes, the mud was sticky. So, all was quiet on the Western Front. Letters or cards for home were the programme. We received parcels and letters. It took five or six days at times to receive them.

Mr. Trenwith sent me a parcel, a lovely thought but it was crushed a bit. I wrote and thanked him and told him not to send me any more because by the time it gets here, the contents are crumbs, mixed and ruined.

I told him we were regularly able to get cigarettes, cigars, cake, biscuits, tins of pears, apricots, peaches and carnation milk, chocolate, spearmint and, most importantly for Jack and Drummy, tripe in Libby's tins with small bottles of vinegar. We could also get Worthington pale ale. I mentioned to Mr. Trenwith that, 'We have already finished off seven barrels of beer from local breweries plus a large barrel of beer from my Battalion race win.' Mr. Trenwith wrote back saying, 'Our Lancashire Fusiliers were very lucky to have commanding officers looking after you.' He understood how I felt and he was relieved to know we didn't need anything. I explained to him that the boys got paid out at every convenient moment when out of the line and all the goods were sold at cost price. They were a lot cheaper than at home and 'all of the best to surprise you, Sir,' I wrote.

A favourite of the men were packets of Huntley and Palmers currant biscuits which were crispy and tasty. Our buyers appreciated it and they knew we sold at cost.

We relied on the 5% discount on our spending to keep buying more stock. Our canteen sold to any unit that passed or was in the vicinity. They would say, 'Cheapest yet.' Even our lads going off on leave, bought some to take home.

Christmas 1917, it's cold and we're on the march

It became cold in November and December. We were in the front line, it was quiet now and it was Christmas Eve 1917. Just as in 1916, we could hear Silent Night being sung by the Germans, this time 150 yards away.

They must have planned it because it sounded loud and there were plenty of singers, not half a dozen in a trench but possibly 50, 60 or even more. It was nice even though it was from the enemy and for 24 hours there was a quiet spell.

We finally left those lines and got down to a rail head after two days marching out of the trenches.

When we left there, it was into the wooded front line at Fonquevillers. It was a place high up and it got shelled more than any I knew both day and night. The Germans did not like us Lancashire Fusiliers of the 10th Battalion.

One night I was set in charge of B Company's ration party. I was down at the dump and waiting for our transport to come. Five limbers arrived and it must have been near midnight.

It was very dark, flares were going up at regular intervals lighting up half a mile or more. When the transport arrived, the German guns were firing shrapnel by the main road. B Company had emptied about half the front limber when one shell dropped in the field twenty yards away and we all ducked down. The two mules in our limber slewed round, got loose and tried to run off back home.

I was in the back half of another limber and, by the time I had jumped up and climbed over the goods or rations, the reins that were on the mules were hanging down. I tried to hold on as we rocked all over the road. The Manchesters transport which was going up about a mile from their dump had pulled up to watch. The mules knew their way and we turned (well, the mules did) into a path and across to our base HQ transport and stores. I pulled up in a lather, quivering. I was sore and bruised but alright.

The transport night duty men took over and transferred the rations into Bob Bateman's two wheeled van. I went back with him after I had hot tea.

The shelling had died down at 2.30am. B Company got their rations and Bob went off back as soon as we unloaded. It was 4am when I got back in the trench, just in time to start another day.

It wasn't double time, just one shilling per day for a Private.

At 6am, I went off to the Forces canteen which was ten miles further down and bought in over 1000 francs worth of stock. Tom Chadwick kept the books straight. Each night, we sorted the takings (cash in hand) and stock so that we were always ready for the boys.

When the Battalion paid out and men visited us, cake was a favourite. It cost five francs to buy. We cut each cake into ten portions, each two and a half inches square. It was a good buy and our lads knew they were getting value for their coppers. When they bought from the Kents, Manchesters and others, it was two pence or three pence extra on everything.

We had 30 packets of spearmint in boxes. At one penny a packet, there was a loss but at one and a half pence per packet we made five pence profit. As I told you, we were selling everything else at as close to cost as possible.

If we were pulled up for selling a blown tin of fruit or anything in a bad condition, it could be weeks or months before we could take it back to the store for an exchange. I told Tom to simply dump all spoiled items.

I never put it in the accounts but I told Tom to always make the accounts balance. If we were cash down, I would make it up with just a franc now and then. The small spearmint profit also pulled the figures up, so it was OK.

That gives you all an idea how our boys got looked after. I bought in biscuits, chocolates, cigarettes, Woodbines in tins of 50. They went in no time.

We also got one tin of tripe in for Jack Hague and Drummy at midnight or 1am or even perhaps 2am, if Jack had just finished his sentry.

Down for leave

Just after Fonquevillers, I was told to go down to base HQ for leave. I was not due for leave this time so first went and bought in some stock that morning to help keep Tom going.

When I arrived at HQ, Sergeant Atherton wanted to confirm my particulars. Private Barny Caine was also down for leave.

In my absence at the stores and knowing my mother's home address, Barny helped the Sergeant and gave him my details on my behalf, 'Sergeant Gregson's address is James Street, West Bank, Widnes, Sir.'

I was actually living with the McKeans at Latchford, Warrington, at the start of the war but I didn't get Atherton to alter it. I would be calling in at home anyway.

Barny Caine, who was from Midwood Street, Simms Cross, Widnes, was ordered to go back to the front line with six to ten others and told to wait for leave this time.

Captain Thompson said to me, 'Caine has asked if you would take his medal that he won for boxing in the Brigade Sports home and call on his family and tell them that he is ok.'

Before Caine left to go back to the front, I said to him, 'You will follow next week, Barny. Wouldn't you like to show it to them yourself?'

'Yes, it would be better.' he agreed and kept hold of it. He wished me a good leave, 'You deserve it.'

Those were his last words to me ever. Whilst at Widnes on one of my days leave, I was going to Moss Bank to visit Lizzy and Uncle Jose Smith when Barny's older brother was coming off shift at 2pm just by Dennis's works. I had already called round on Sunday afternoon and told them all about Barny's bout that he had won and about life over there, in general.

Barny's brother pulled me up, 'Sergeant, did you hear about poor Barny?'

'No' I replied.

'He got killed returning back to the trenches.' I asked him how he knew so quickly and he said from a letter from Private Harry something (I am sorry his name won't come at the moment).

The Commonwealth Graves Commission's records show that, 'Private 5297 Bernard Caine, son of Andrew and Catherine Caine of 4

Travis Street, Widnes, died on 26th March 1918, and is Remembered with Honour at the Arras Memorial.'

It is hard for me to remember all the names. I remember the ones who made an outstanding impact on me. Now, I will tell you what Caine giving my Widnes address did for me. Poor Caine could not possibly have known that fourteen days leave at Widnes, got me 28 all told.

My mother hadn't had enough even with 6 sons and 4 daughters. Dad died in February 1916 as I told you when I was in Dartford. Mum took in a baby boy whose mother had neglected him. She had been going drinking and leaving him to the mercy of anybody.

Mother signed for him and christened him William (Billy) Gregson. Whilst I was home, Billy got measles and the doctor sent me to The Peninsula Barracks, South Lancashire Depot. The doctor there asked if I would be in contact with food, canteen work. That did it, extra leave!

He told me that my mother's doctor would decide when to send me back.

If I had given my Warrington address instead of Barny giving my Widnes address, this wouldn't have happened. I was now at the same address as a boy (William) with measles. So, I was lucky missing two drafts. Barny was unlucky missing his draft. The French would say, 'C'est la guerre.'

When I did get back to our base, it was early morning, Captain 'Tiddles' Thompson, the Quartermaster, was walking about looking for metal and anything else he could salvage. When he was salvaging, he would say, 'Sergeant, pick that shell case up and put it with this junk.' He hadn't time to salute back. With his short cane tucked up under his arm pit, he would wag it to say, 'Pick that and pick this, stoop down, Gregson.'

Running the canteen was hard work. Sometimes the British Expeditionary Forces canteen moved. It had to as it belonged to the 17th Division and moved with it.

A brick-setter got a permanent job down at the base building cooking ovens and fireplaces for cooking purposes. He got the bricks from knocked down buildings. Bricks, mud, iron bars, rails; he was able to use them all. There were joiners who made bedposts to hold hammocks and made repairs. If you were handy building or could do something useful down the base, you would stay there.

Amongst the chaos of war, there was time for running – I did what I was told!

After two nights and days of making new trenches and communication trenches, I got orders to leave the line and go down to our base to travel to a sports ground.

The 17th Division was holding a sports meeting and Colonel Torrens had entered me into the mile race.

Now, this was a nightmare. I got orders just before dusk that I had to go out immediately and stay the remainder of the night in the transport camp, out of those trenches over to some gun pits that were firing away. There I stopped and enquired my way to Toutenwood.

I had to go under a bridge which the Germans were shelling and half knocked down an officer.

I got a drink, and had a talk to the Sergeant who had a watch. He was counting how many seconds and minutes between each shell at that bridge. Finally, the Sergeant said, 'It's fully 100 yards to the road under that bridge so when I say go, you must run to get under and away. But take cover as soon as possible.'

I got up ready. We heard the shell going. 'Go!' yelled the Sergeant and I moved off before the explosion. All sorts flew up. I got under there, round and down.

I got four hours sleep, then had breakfast and got on my way to go six miles more. After two, I got a lift in a limber with a Gloucesters unit. I then had one mile to walk across an old battleground, jumping old trenches and dug outs and everything else in my way.

I got there in time to get No. 1 cards put on my back and front. I didn't know anything about the race, including who I was racing, what the race was or why we were running.

A red capped Captain told us it was just five laps for a mile with the bell to ring for the last lap.

One Sergeant shouted, 'Hey Albert, Sergeant Gregson is running.'

'Right,' was the reply. It turned out to be Corporal A.G. Hill, the English four-mile champion. It was his unit, the Aviation Corps Observation Balloon section that was located nearby.

He sought me out and said, 'Glad to meet you, Sergeant.' It was then he told me who he was, as if it mattered. It was war, day and night whether you were a Private or a General. We were all one of a cog in a wheel helping out. I was Alf Gregson, it made no difference.

The officials put us two together at the start by the line.

Hill asked, 'How do you run your race?' I said, 'From the gun.'

I don't know whether he thought I was sarcastic or not. I had an idea why I had been thrown in this race. He was trained and ready for a good trial. I had just left the line with four hours sleep, dodging shells to get to the sports ground and then had to run. Him, there with his balloon on the same ground!

We were off, with a bang.

I went straight in the lead of the twenty runners, Hill was behind me. On the first four laps, it was just the same, he never tried to pass. At the bell for the last lap, I was faster. I knew it was shorter than a lap. The first four laps were 440 yards each, the fifth was 350 yards.

Well, I knew I could knock the stuffing out of anyone. I ran a quick pace for the whole mile and it was a sprint finish. However, today I wasn't good and when he tried to pass with 100 yards to go, I held him off and we were going faster and as fast as I could go. I was tired when he came past rolling with five yards to go. He won.

Afterwards down on the field, he was sat with head and shoulders forward down between his knees. I picked up my coat and got a big surprise. An announcement was made, 'Will the second, third and fourth runners in that mile race, come over at once for their prizes.'

I got 140 francs.

The red cap informed me that Corporal Hill wasn't in our division so was not eligible for the prize. He was training for the English Mile Championship. I was thrilled with my luck but I felt I was there for people to command, do this and do that. I was being ordered what to do. That race was got up for Hill with mostly officers running and all officers officiating.

The War Diary notes on the 4th July 1918 at Toutencourt Woods,
'Early parade at 6:30am. Usual training in the morning. Divisional HQ Sports during the afternoon. In the open mile race, Sergeant Gregson, the

Battalion representative ran second, being beaten by half-a-lap by Air Mechanic Hill, who however was not available for the prize.'

When I was going across the field, I walked into a Warrington officer. He had been transferred to a Labour Corps. He was Lieutenant Reuben Bennett. I think he was a Wesleyan General Insurance official back home.

I do know that in 1913, he was a club runner. I had done a bit with him. He had been a good 120 to 220 yards sprinter and sometimes a 440 yards runner. He was, like me, a Warrington AC member.

He said he had come to see the race. I told him all about it, from the time I left the line until I met him. He said it was the ground where he wanted to run a sports meeting, in four days time for 120 men in his Company. It was nice to have a chat even if it was on a balloon field and not in a cafe or an estaminet. I had six miles to go so we parted and we didn't meet again in France.

When I gave Colonel Torrens my account of the race, he said, 'Never mind Sergeant you got two days less in the line.'

'Yes, and I missed twelve hours sleep, dodging shells' I replied.

He only smiled.

As I got to the tent flap, he said, 'You have told me about the prizes but was there any betting?'

'No, Sir, there was only one race and that was for A.G. Hill.'

I get myself into a spot of bother

We had a spell or two in and out of the Green line in and around Arras. One warm and sunny afternoon, we had some time off.

I asked if anyone fancied a swim. Ten Privates, a Lance Corporal and I got our towels and went over our camping ground to the River Scarpe. Round a bend it flowed cleanly for about 25 to 30 yards with thick bushes and trees on the opposite bank.

We swam across and played about for an hour and then ran wild to dry ourselves. We rubbed ourselves down and walked back for tea and into trouble.

The orderly (who do you think? Sergeant Jack Heitman!) said, 'Greg, you and your 'Channel' swimmers are for orders when your B Company gets back. The Chinese have killed a Yank.' At 6pm, I had to see the Captain for 'Leaving camp without orders.' Punishment? 'At once, collect your swimmers and rating and for three days, guard those Chinese.'

Now believe me, when that motor stopped at their guard room at Arras, the Chinese officer shook me by the hand. 'Verly Wecom, Sergeant,' he said. That Lieutenant could speak English very well. They had their own guard as well as ours. I had bought in 200 francs worth of stock for the Chinese and everything was emptied from our motor transport and was carried into a scrubbed hut with chairs, tables, bunk beds, coat hooks, all made in camp by the Chinese. We got a cup of tea straight away.

We didn't see where the bacon, cheese, meat, beans, bread, bully, tins of tomatoes, tea, sugar and tinned milk went.

They laid the tables with toast, bacon, tomatoes and bread. There was plenty of tea and milk and it was good. We seemed to get a better ration than we did with the Battalion. We had the best three days of the war with no trouble, plenty of dominoes, draughts and cards. They waited on us and they even polished our boots. They were sorry when we went.

Nice boys, we were told we were, 'not like those bullies the Yanks. They kick us out of the road when that day they marched past. One Yank knocked a Chinese man out with a blow and then kicked him, one of my men hit him with a spade. He die. Now court martial for my man.' They said, 'We will have to shoot the Yanks if they come again for a fight.'

I had bought cigarettes, biscuits and cake from the Forces canteen for that party of Chinese who had looked after us. They liked that.

Our Captain said, 'That will teach you a lesson, Sergeant,'

'Yes, Sir,' and I wished it could have been a longer punishment!

We went out of shape eating rice puddings, not in rations, and tea between meals late at night.

When we returned, our Battalion moved up for a spell of eight days. The Germans made a raid but it failed.

B Company had dug a trench straight out towards the Germans and were in it when Jerry came over. The Germans got caught from their flank and front, got confused and retreated with losses. When we went out of the line, it was to the same camp by the river.

Whilst buying in, I spotted 29th Division transport. I asked them where their camp was, 'St Catherines, north of Arras.' I got back and asked permission to go over to see if I could find my old 1st Battalion platoon Lieutenant 'Rochdale'. To cut the story, the platoon had got ordered to march. When I got near, I followed and looking at every officer until I reached the Lieutenant. I wanted to talk about Lew Knowles and Paddy Murphy from Gallipoli.

He recognised me but he had to shout, 'See me when we come out.'

He never did. When I went back they told me a shell had exploded in the road and killed the Lieutenant and the Sergeant leading up with him so I don't know what happened to Lew and Paddy. The Lieutenant got away from Gallipoli to France but went no further.

Grand weather in August 1918 and I'm running again

The weather was grand. It was now August 1918.

We were out for changes, rest and play. The Manchesters were to hold a sports day with a special mile race and not just for their Battalion.

All in the 17th Division who could possibly get to the village could compete. That included us as we were only three miles away.

I was on good form. After the Artillery mile, we had camped as you know (when I got punished for swimming) on the field by the Scarpe. It had been good level grassland so I had taken advantage to do some training. 'Be Prepared,' Baden Powell said and he was a Boer War officer.

I had a few days easy and three or four days for running, walking, baths with plenty of water and helpers with rubbing down.

It struck me funny that bets were taking place between officers and the 'Happies' (the Manchester's nickname was the 'Happy Dan's).

Sergeant Jack Heitman through Company Sergeant Major Moody of D Company (Moody was from Halebank, Widnes) got to know the Manchesters had been reinforced and a Corporal Thomas had joined them. Thomas was a good miler and had never been beaten either at home or abroad since 1914 with different Manchester units.

It goes to say Heitman, Moody and Company Sergeant Major Toms all went over to the race ground on Sunday. They got in their Sergeant mess and took bets at 2-1.

I thought he must be a good runner or else he hadn't run against anybody of any quality. When I raced with A.G. Hill, our time was 4 minutes 12 seconds but I didn't take it because there was no serious timing with any watch with a second hand and not too particular measurements. It wouldn't have been longer than a mile and, actually, could have been shorter.

I gave Jack Hague 70 francs to put on the tote, 50 for myself and 20 for Jack.

Sergeant Heitman running his Crown and Anchor Housey House, as it was called in those days, took bets if any one fancied Thomas.

Major Forwood told me, just as I got to the tent where we were to change, that he had got 100 francs at 2-1 with a Kent Commanding officer. 'They have a Captain who will win.'

So, the Kents, the Manchesters and the Engineers Sergeant were all backed.

It was funny when I got inside the tent when I asked the Captain, a Manchester (well, he had Mancs badges so I assumed he was), for my two cards with my running number on each card. He said, 'Sergeant, are you superstitious? Your number is thirteen.'

'No, Sir, I have won with number thirteen and it was for a gold chain.'

He said 'I'll only be a minute.' I watched him go into the next tent, place a bet and come trotting back. He just winked, I didn't nosey. It could have been for me or it could be for Corporal Thomas (Manchesters).

Our faithful 50 or more men, not including the Lancashire Fusiliers HQ staff and all the officers from A, B, C and D Companies, Whitworth, Newman and Toms, were all in a happy mood.

The Manchesters' Sergeants' Mess had whisky and Worthington Pale Ale on sale during the meeting from 11am until 4 pm.

I looked up the runners on a sheet pinned on the tent pole. Thomas's number was 18 so I went out to look for that card. He was very strong if his build was anything to go by. He had dark hair and a look of tan, fresh air and sun. He had a red and white hooped rugby top. At the start, there were nineteen runners. We had four laps to run, three laps then the bell.

During the race, I had him in view. He sprinted.

I couldn't let Thomas go too far without doing something. So, I got into a pace that I knew I could stick with and gained some back. We had finished the first lap, it was a fast race. He was either very good or he was chancing me packing up, running us all off our legs to catch him. Two laps gone and I was twenty yards behind Thomas with half a mile to go. At the bell, it was 75 yards. In the next 440 yards, I was going as I started, fast but not sprinting. He was tiring and his backers were cheering, yelling and shouting at him to keep at it for ten yards and two more bends and then a 70 yard straight finish. When the difference was down to five yards, I sprinted all I could, all out, and I won by ten yards.

Our crowd ran in and got hold of me to carry me up. Company Sergeant Major Toms, with his strong voice, told them not to, 'You might hurt him, let him get his wind back, go and get your winnings.'

Our HQ Commanding Officer Wade was waving. Colonel Torrens, Major Forwood, all of them were in good cheer.

The Commanding Officer from the 10th Manchesters handed 168 francs to me saying, 'Sergeant, you ran a good, well-judged race. It looked at one time too much for even you, if I may say so. I, with pleasure present you with your first prize, a packet containing one hundred, one fifty and a ten franc note and eight francs in three notes.'

The tote paid three to one so I got 150 francs winnings from the tote. Jack Hague got 60 francs winnings. He wouldn't have his stake. 'Sorry, it wasn't mine,' he said, 'no.'

I got back in that tent when I could get free.

The Manchesters Canteen Sergeant who I knew well said his Regimental Sergeant Major would like to see me. I, with Sergeant Jack went to the mess, which was in an estaminet.

I was congratulated by all from the Regimental Sergeant Major, Regimental Quartermaster down to the Sergeant. 'A grand race to watch,' they said. They supplied me with salad sandwiches and pale ale at their expense.

About five Lancashires (Toms, Whitworth, Company Quartermaster Harvey, Jack and I) stayed for half an hour and then left.

They wanted us to stay. 'I will put on transport tonight.' I told Jack Heitman that he could please himself. I left and Jack said he would walk back slowly, now it was nice and warm.

Some Corporals and Privates had waited for us to come out. They had been in the same estaminet but not in the side that was the Sergeants' mess. They'd been able to buy all sorts as they had all won. It was a 30 minute walk back for tea though some went to the estaminet in our village instead. I didn't do so badly with my winnings. Happy Dans or was it Happy Lancs?

I hope you all understand it all.

I write as I saw it acted and putting it in words something like it was spoken at the time.

Another day to be remembered, helping a French family

The 10th Battalion Lancashire Fusiliers were lucky to have sportsmen at the head. We were ordered to go in on the right of Cambrai with rushes through Inchy and Beaumont, half a mile beyond.

Our canteen, with Tom and Bill, was located in the ruins of a house by the main street. I took a look round in the house just off the main road. I heard shouts and two small boys came trotting up to me. 'Soldat,' they said in French. They got hold of my hand and pulled at me. They took me down into a cellar where there were three women, a mother and two daughters. One of the girls, Isabelle, was sickly and was wounded in the shoulder. They all had a touch of gas. I knew where our doctor's dug out was so I ran to it. I told Sergeant Harold Nolan, one of those kinds of chaps where nothing was trouble. He was a Salford man and he was young, very clean with a fresh complexion. Straightaway, he got out a doctor's bag and put things in it. The doctor was shaving himself at the tap in the back when he heard and shouted to mix a bottle for the sickness. I told him where they were, 'Up this street at the top towards our Battalion.' Harold rushed ahead and the boys, who were about four and six, were waiting. I'd told them I would bring the doctor. They shouted, 'Allez, doctor.'

Harold gave the woman and girls a dose of something in a small measure. Then we put Isabelle on a bed mattress that we had brought down into the cellar. Harold did all he could by the time Smith (our Captain doctor) arrived. Captain Smith was no-nonsense. If you were half dead, he would give you medicine and tell you it was your duty to carry on. He never had a queue like Captain Thomas had! When Captain Smith had to go, I told them I would call back an hour later.

Charlie Hales, always known as 'Cheeky' was a good hearted chap, and Bob Martin, his mate, were both cooks and Wiganers. They had got some hot soup with bread for the family. Our B Company cooking kitchen was only 100 yards away in the village. I told Tom and Bill that we needed spearmint for those boys and chocolate biscuits for the ladies. Georgette was the youngest, twelve, and Isabelle was fifteen. She was asleep when I called with the goodies. She had soup then fell off to sleep again.

Harold also promised to call back at 3pm, so they would be all right now. The cooks, the doctor and the canteen hands meant that one French family would be looked after. The village looked deserted. When I called at tea time, the older woman had something to eat. I brought a tin of coffee, the Red White Blue brand. I also left a tin of carnation milk and some sugar from Charlie the cook.

We had digging and other work to do for two days; it was called 'consolidating our position.' The weather was at its best. Then, our Battalion moved up, the Essex's took over our position. The Vendegies-au-Bois family would now have the Essex's doctor to take the place of Harold and Doctor Smith. I left biscuits and pears, milk and chocolate but I couldn't do anything else and they could look after themselves and Isabelle.

We took over the trenches on the right of Cambrai which was getting it hot and was on fire. We twice had to repel German attacks which we did but with casualties.

After a week, we were taken out and into camp trenches just short of Caudry. I bought in at our Forces canteen in Caudry. It was the nearest I ever had to travel to buy in, usually I'd have to travel five to ten miles.

At about 7pm, our postman, Corporal Holden had finished his collection ready for morning and he asked me to go with him to look round the town. I had already been in town buying in the morning.

We went by a lane alongside a row of houses. 'Let's knock and ask for coffee, Sergeant.' Holden said.

At the first door, there was no answer. Second door, third door, no answer but, at the fourth, a tall lady peeped out of a partly opened door, 'Coffee Madame?' Holden asked.

"No, no, monsieurs. Pas de cafe.'

Holden insisted on a coffee. Her husband opened the door wide. 'Entrez, soldiers,' he said. 'Sergeant,' he continued and he took me to the cupboard and put an inch square of fat on a piece of bread about the size of a half, small Hovis loaf, only it was dark, almost black, and stale.

I was sorry and disappointed with Holden who was still asking for coffee. 'Come Posty, these people have nothing to sell or to give', I said.

'No, they hide. I'll wait Sergeant.'

'You will be on your own if you don't come.' I told him. When I got outside, I waited for him to come. When he didn't, I went back to Tom and Bill.

Bill put into a clean, new sandbag a tin of pears, milk, biscuits, cigarettes, matches, candles, chocolate, coffee and cake. Tom jotted it all down. Then, I took it to Cheeky Charlie and Bob Martin, the B Company cooks, and told them all about the walk with Holden.

He said, 'I am more surprised you go out with that scrounger.' I told them it was the first and it would be the last time. I asked them for some sugar, bread and some cheese if they could spare it. I then went over to Sergeant Swash, the HQ Caterer, and asked him to spare four bottles of pale ale, two of stout and the six bottles at his expense. He agreed, saying it was my turn to be treated, 'It's been you who treated our HQ and staff. We all did well with the Happy Dans (meaning their winnings at the Manchesters' Mile).'

When I got back, the cooks had attached the two sandbags together and I offered them two bottles of pale ale each but they didn't want any. I had to leave one each behind.

Then, I went back to the house and Holden was still there, sat up to the fire stove talking and trying to speak French, not successfully, to their daughter, Naomi.

I went with the mother to the cupboard and put in what I had got from Tom and Charlie. We gave them about half a pound of bacon and half a pound of cheese, a loaf, sugar, tea, each in a linen bag. Two nice thin slices of beef (steak), a tin of dripping and salt.

Without anyone seeing, I went back and asked the daughter to put some water on and I pulled from my pockets two Worthington pale ales and two Guinnesses. I opened two currant biscuits, large ones. I encouraged them to use carnation milk with tea. They were a bit doubtful about tea but liked it when they tasted it sweetened. They asked if they could share another. I said it was all theirs. The mother cried and the dad couldn't speak. Naomi was busy giving out biscuits which they liked, believe me.

They would have been happy with bread and butter and nothing else. I gave Holden a cup of tea and told him that all the other things were for people who had been on a starvation diet for three and a half years, not like us. On the way home, I told him that this was the last time I'd go out for a wander with him. All he said was, 'How was I to know.' I didn't argue with him.

I called next morning early. I was in time to cook two breakfasts for the dad and mum. The daughter was washing up and helping out at the YMCA for the troops. I cooked bacon with tinned tomatoes and bread. I got it just right. Then we made two rounds of toast with butter and a jar of marmalade. Tom had put coffee into the bag (it was all coffee in France). Dad said he liked tea but preferred coffee. They thanked me. Mother got busy with the dishes although I could see no soap just sand, dry in a tin box with plenty of water from the well. The water was nice and cool. I tasted it.

In touch with Home

I got back to answering letters from Widnes, Warrington, Barrow, Birmingham and elsewhere. I also wrote to Mrs. Needham, the wife of my old platoon's Lieutenant from the 1st Battalion in Gallipoli who took me with him to shoot that Turk the first morning in a trench.

She had sent me a parcel. It was the second that she had sent to me. On the first occasion, she wrote a note saying, 'My husband wrote and told me about you and your family. I pray for your mother with five sons out on active service. She must be proud of you all. It is hoped she will be spared the pain that I have to bear.' I wrote and thanked her and I shared it with a few who never got parcels.

Some of the men never got a card, nothing, and I never asked why. The parcels that were received by those that got them, often included food, chocolate and cigarettes and very often they arrived in a broken state and it was such a shame.

The men could actually get all we wanted, fresh at cost and the boys were all well in credit. Two, three weeks in credit sometimes.

There was no pay up in the line but they would buy in beforehand – cigarettes, spearmint and biscuits to put in their packs.

I could send home the same foods such as chocolate, cake cigarettes. Then they would see for themselves the state it would be in.

Well, we just rested, just a matter of roll call, washing, shaving, cleaning boots and buttons and badges when we were on active service. It was handy for me that week as it only took me ten minutes to get to the British Expeditionary Forces canteen.

I also called at the house to see if I could do something for Naomi's family. They wanted to buy bully beef. I got six tins, I scrounged them from Sergeant Jack, Jack Hague, Tom, Bill and myself. We could replace them. When we were in the trench, it was our own to eat. If we had the food too long, we had it changed. It was dumped by us before it did get old. We got fresh from our iron rations.

It was back to the front next night so Tom and Bill were busy giving the boys their requirements.

The dad said, 'Moi payez, Sergeant, maintenant.'

I said 'Where do you get money?'

'Naomi work now.'

I told him his comrade 'donne' and was glad to do so. I called at 5pm the next night as we had to fall in at 6pm. Mum and dad kissed me on both cheeks and mum cried quietly. Naomi was at work at the YMCA. We all understood a lot without having to speak.

Later on in August 1918, we were back to the front.

Back to the front

Back, this time two miles on the right front of Cambrai. It was still smoking and there were flames with a few shells going in. It rained all night. Ground sheets were worn by those on duty, like I was. Some battery of ours was dropping shells too near our trench – ten yards just in front.

I rushed to our platoon Lieutenant Delmer and told him those shells were dropping too near our lines, 'something was wrong.' They were 100 yards or more short if it was the German trench they wanted. Delmer got our HQ to send some flares up as an S.O.S. to lift their range.

An artillery Captain came along our trench and wanted to know exactly where the nearest shells landed. I soon showed him, five lots at ten yards which was the nearest and some at twenty yards, the furthest. We went out front and came back, it was dark. Anyway, we had no more near us after that.

A Company made a raid and took seven prisoners, a Corporal and six Privates, young ones, just in the line. They had been rushed up from another front. Now it wasn't the amount of prisoners that mattered, it was who, when and where and from which front they were taken.

The weather got warmer but damp. After a good spell of 'feelers' (company advances), we captured 30 Germans and 200 yards of ground without much opposition although one Sergeant was killed and five men were wounded from our B Company. Those Germans looked in poor shape and didn't show much heart for fighting. Some were already with their hands up shouting 'Komrad!'

Our Regimental Sergeant Major Newman could speak German so he came in handy and he got to know a lot. He got to know why we hadn't much trouble taking them prisoners. They had been ordered to hold on whilst the main troops got back to new positions. So, we made another quick advance in the dusk with dirty, dark faces.

The Guards took over and by the time they went over the top, it was to meet stiff opposition. They got back to where they came from with losses. We got down to our old reserve trench near Inchy Beaumont.

Isabelle was doing fine, walking about now. Two units had been billeted in Inchy since we left. So, they had been looked after by doctors. They were glad to see me but we didn't stay long.

I went over to Caudry and the Germans had retreated a mile or so. It meant all troops moved up, so we went. I looked in to give a few biscuits, cigarettes and chocolates at both houses. I had an idea it would be for the last time.

We started a big offensive from the Cambrai area. Our troops seemed to advance, taking prisoners. The prisoners looked a mixed lot, young, old, tired, dirty, some wounded. They had first aid and some were helping to support others to the concentration camps.

We were moving up each day following the Kents. When they came out, the Manchesters were going in. We then took over after the Dans. We had the Germans giving ground along a big front.

The German planes dropping bombs were not so accurate, kind of 'drop and get away.' We rushed on but all we captured was about six

Germans with a few bombs. We called them 'Tater Mashers'. They were nothing like our Mills bombs.

The prisoners were glad to be taken. They had been left behind to bomb and machine gun us all.

When our platoon went over throwing bombs, the Germans were crouching down covering up for fear of being hit. They were jumping down in the hurriedly made trench (more like a dry ditch) shouting 'Komrad!' They didn't fire at us. As said, Newman got to know that they had orders to hold our troops up for as long as possible. But they knew the main German troops had been withdrawn in motors and rushed back to some trenches made for them to retire to. They were good trenches.

We were still going on slowly but surely. We got held up, not on our Lancashire Fusiliers front, but away on the right flank. So, the centre (that was us) had to wait for orders.

The weather was kind to us and the going was getting better. We came across big guns that had been put out of action or hit by our bombs from our planes or a direct hit from our long range guns. It was not long before we reached them.

There were dead still there. We had time to bury them and put something sticking up to say when, who and which regiment. We got all this from their pay books, letters, photographs and anything else they might have on them.

For a month, we didn't need to go down or out, we inter-changed with other troops so we got to sleep at night.

We just had sentries posted to waken us if we were wanted.

The Germans were quite on the run now and prisoners came in steadily.

We advanced on into open country, until we got held up for 24 hours. The Germans had managed to entrench and hold us up but, after a couple of days, our extreme flanks had almost surrounded them so they got going back again.

All this was round about September 1918. Every day, we were going a few miles with just pockets of machine gun nests and long range guns firing a few shots. We would then drop back again. We got nights of seven or eight hours sleep. Then, onto hills and farms which had been German strongholds. Our guns spared buildings of all kinds now.

The farm hands would meet us. They had dug out wine and other provisions from somewhere that they had hidden from the Germans. If our platoon of about 56 men got to a farm or village, we slept in schools or barns. On and on we went with not much doing with us. A fresh unit in motor transport was going on fast and told us we had the Germans on the way back to Berlin.

We had a long range firing gun, a Big Bertha with a girl's name (Lizzy, Anne, Ruth?) chalked on the side. Once the gun had fired, it would be packed up and go on, passing us again. We halted for dinner with our Battalion, the old 10th Lancashire Fusiliers, once again all together. Our transport with us in our rear. We were cooking on the march.

The end is nigh!

My war recollections are coming to a close. It was November 4th 1918. We got to a farm that we called German Petticoat Farm. It was our B Company billet for the night.

On 3rd November, the War Diary documented, *'During the morning, verbal orders were received that the Battalion would attack through the Foret de Mormal & capture the line, S.9.c.5.0 – S.15.a.8.0*

At dusk, Battalion HQ moved up to Petit Gay Farm and all preparations for the attack in the morning were completed, advanced posts being slightly withdrawn in order to escape our own barrage.

On the 4th, the Diary continues, *'The Battalion assembled on a general line X.17.b.60.95, X.17.d.95.60 in the following order: C & D Company from right to left in front with B & A Company in close support.*

At 05:30 hours, the barrage opened & remained on enemy front line for four minutes when the Battalion attacked, each Company being on a 2 platoon frontage with 2 in close support. Day broke about 05:45 with an extremely heavy ground mist. Little opposition was encountered up to the copse, X.18.a.5.8, which D Company quickly rushed & captured the Garrison. C Company on the right first encountered resistance in copse S.13.d. The 2 leading platoons succeeded in rushing the posts & pushed on towards Futoy.

At 06:06 hours, the Louvigines Road was reached, the left leading Company passing La Motte Farm a few minutes later, leaving its support Company to mop up. At this time heavy Machine Gun fire was encountered from the farm building. Lewis Guns were brought into action & one platoon detailed to rush the farm.

The remainder of the Company moved to the east side of the buildings & were in time to capture several of the enemy emerging from an outhouse. No difficulties were experienced in helping close up to the barrage & the advance was now fairly rapid. Opposition from the western edge of Futoy was overcome by leading Company and after the barrage had lifted from the line of the road – S.14.a & c. – the advance continued.

Immediately, after the support Company had crossed the road & mopped up the village, the enemy barrage (which had been previously falling in vicinity of jumping off positions) came down on the road.

Futoy was captured at 07:05 hours.

Hostile artillery activity was now increasing, and sides and tracks were severely searched. Companies reached the final objective at 08:00 hours & immediately consolidated east of this line.

Platoon posts were formed & the left support Company established an International post at cross roads S.8.c.9.1. Whilst digging in Companies were subjected to shelling from the left & desultory Machine Gun fire from North of Pont A Vache. The protective barrage remained for 30 minutes to enable the 51st Brigade to form up & pass through, followed later by the 50th Brigade.

The 52nd Brigade was now in Divisional Reserve, the Battalion moving into billets in Futoy in the evening.

In the yard, there were 200 or more prisoners. Some Scottish Regiment was with them, they were to rest for the night. Two big barns with straw were handy for all.

There was a shell for what seemed like every 30 minutes.

As I told you, our Regimental Sergeant Major Newman was a London Police Sergeant, and with his knowledge of German, he was in his element. He was finding out the when, where, why, and who. When the very last shell was heard in that 'War game', I was with Charlie Newman and he was telling me what the Jerries had told him. They were glad to pack up. They had had no real food and they were stealing it. They were tired, foot sore and going back on foot with The Tommies rushing fast towards them. They threw all their uniforms away and their rifles and bombs and they turned and gave up. They were glad to have finished with war.

Well, Newman and I were talking when the last shell hit the big gable end of the barn and all of us ducked down. I was knocked unconscious and only woke at 3am. I awoke to hear Sergeant Harold Nolan with Doctor Smith who was asking, 'A packet of biscuits, Sergeant?'

They had a farmyard oil lamp which lit Newman and I could see his arm in a sling, broken. My head, nose and chin were all bandaged up. It was now 5pm on November 4th and it was almost a birthday gift. Tomorrow was November 5th and I was to be 29. 'You look younger than that,' they were saying. 'You can't beat the time you were born,' and I stated clearly, 'I was born in Widnes in 1889.'

I favoured a 'Father Christmas' head with eyes, nose and chin bandaged and now I only needed a bag of toys! Sergeant Jack Heitman heard that Sergeant Gregson and the Regimental Sergeant Major had been hit. He had been around but D Company was a mile away from where we were billeted in a large village away from any shelling, lucky D Company.

They would have to search the houses and the villagers helped. They knew who would have Germans.

We carried on each morning following up. We only stopped for a rest, then dinner, rest, off again, then put up for the night. We didn't have or hear any more shells.

On the 8th November, the War Diary stated, *'The Battalion moved to Aulnoye, staying in billets until evening, when orders were issued for a further attack. Consequently, the Battalion moved about 22:30 hours to Limonte Fontaine to relieve the 7th Lincolns. The objective being the village of Beaufort. The march up was exceedingly quiet, not a shell from the enemy being heard. On arrival at Limonte Fontaine, information was received that the enemy had withdrawn, & that one Company of the 7th Lincolns, following up the enemy, had established itself in Beaufort. A Company was now detailed as advance guard to the Battalion & proceeded to Beaufort finding no sign of the enemy. The other 3 Companies now followed and an outpost line was established about 1 mile east of the village, with B Company as outpost Company, A & D Companies forming a defensive flank on the left with C Company in support.*

At 8am, on the 9th, Cavalry patrols were pushed through the outpost line, but were unable to make contact with the enemy. And at 15:00, in the afternoon, A, C & D Companies were withdrawn to billets in the village. B Company remaining on the outpost line.'

Continuing into the 10th November at 6am, the Diary recorded, *'D Company relieved B Company in the outpost line, B Company moving back into the village.'*

On the night of the 10th of November, we arrived at a nice size village called Beaufort. Their church steeple had a shell hole made through it, in the front and out the back.

I had killed the two occupants a week before the 11th November when Jerry was firing long range shots, it was hit and run. We patrolled the streets and searched. The villagers told us the 'Soldat' had 'regardez', looked around and found three Germans wounded. Our B Company slept in a large barn. I was in the bay by the farm gate, only ten yards from the road.

At 8am on November 11th, according to the War Diary, *'Wire received stating that the enemy had agreed to the conditions of the armistice as laid down by the Allies & that hostilities would cease at 11:00 hours today. About 12:30 hours, the Battalion moved to Berlaimont, this being the first stage of the journey back to Inchy.'*

It was 4am when I heard shouting and a knock on the gate. 'Open up, someone,' I heard. I got my pants, tunic and boots on and opened the gate which was bolted top and bottom.

'It's Sergeant Gregson?'

'Yes, Sir.' I replied. It was our Commanding Officer Colonel Torrens, 'Good news I bring, Sergeant. I heard this very morning, the armistice will be signed.'

'Well, by 'eck,' I said.

'You don't seem pleased, Gregson.' Torrens said.

He went to tell our Captain Pegrum. I went up to the farmhouse door and a French farmer came. Our Colonel spoke French and soon the Captain came. He got orders to have his Company march down to the Church in clean, walking out dress, no equipment but polished, shaved and smart as all units within our area were to attend. Torrens told Pegrum that I wasn't pleased with it. 'Why?' my Captain said.

'When we had them ready for a knock out beat, he is getting away with it,' I said.

'Come on, Sergeant, close that gate after me.'

He was on horseback and when he got through he looked at me

closing the gate. Then he said, 'You have been a good fighter, Gregson, I suppose the 1st Battalion 29th Division taught you.'

'No, Sir. The owd tenth', that is, the 10th Battalion Lancashire Fusiliers.'

He galloped on, I suppose to tell the others. He had been at the Division HQ all night and was telling our Battalion the news and their orders.

At 10.30am, all were on parade. On the church steps, there were padres from all denominations. Our Divisional Chaplain was Church of England and he gave the service, singing hymns, a sermon, more hymns and at, 11am, there was five minutes silence. I suppose signing the armistice was taking place.

We then marched back for early dinner and twelve hours leave in the villages until 12am.

I had a day with Sergeant Jack Heitman and Sergeant Harold Nolan. We didn't drink much; a couple of dashes was enough till tea at 4.30pm. If you wanted to go back for it, there was bread, butter and jam.

Cheeky Charlie Hales gave us three rounds of beef dripping on bread fried in a roasting tin until it was just brown. We ate with a knife, a fork, a plate and some sauce. All of it was supplied in his farm yard shelter. It was accompanied by strong tea with farm milk. Jack Heitman had bought six eggs and, in a mess tin lid, fried them. Two each on our fried rounds, it was the first tasty tea I had ever had since we rested at Doullens.

We walked back to Beaufort, had a look round then sorted out a fresh estaminet with music going on.

A Corporal from D Company was playing all sorts, just what came into his head, marches, waltzes and songs. An Engineer Sergeant sang along to them but we joined in. By that time, they were merry.

The local French people were mainly elderly men. There were not many of them and they were farmers who had been in German hands from 1914–1918. They were shouting, 'La Guerre finis', 'War Finish Now', 'Vive Angleterre', 'Francaise' and they were singing 'Mademoiselle from Armentiers Parlez Vous' and other tunes until it was time to get a good night's sleep.

At 9am breakfast, we had bacon, egg and toast. We paid extra for some nice things when we could get them. Sergeant Swash of the HQ

Catering looked after that. There were tins of tomatoes, sausage, extra cheese, eggs and french bread, when it was possible.

Going Back home? Maybe or maybe not

Now it was a case of going back, which meant weeks of marching. Transport was needed for the troops who had to go into Germany to dump off iron rations and shells etc and to make sure all sorts were cleaned up.

The War Diary noted on 13th November to the 26th November, *'Battalion completed the march to Inchy via Ollivers Ameral remaining there for the rest of the month. Whilst at Inchy, salvage work was energetically carried out, at least one Company per day being always employed. Many kinds of sport were organised including football matches, paper chases etc.'*

Our Battalion were on our way back. We filled a big hole in a main road so transport could get on to it and save themselves going miles out of their way. It took twelve hours. It looked like a small fishing pond but it was deep. It took four limbers going back and to for 20 or 30 minutes at a time. We were filling the limbers and others were emptying them into the crater which had been made by a direct hit from a plane. It looked like it was old earth around the hole.

I got to the camp and we had a week's complete rest with nothing to do apart from being on parade for 9am each morning. Now, it was shave, buttons etc treated to 'spit and polish' and equipment washed.

There had been a reinforcement to camp with fresh soldiers from England who would report first at the YMCA before being sent to their units.

We got 'Blanco' for our equipment and there was Guard Duty as well. We marched on and on and, on December 5th, we got settled in a lovely village called Vergies.

The War Diary states on the 12th December, *'The last days march was now commenced via Soves & Airaines. D Company whose destination was Havrincourt reached there about 14:00 hours whilst the rest of the Battalion went on to Vergies. The whole march was exceedingly well done, only seven failing to finish mainly owing to sickness.*

Work was very quickly started on the billets which required a certain amount of attention. Huts were also constructed, the first one being the men's recreation room.

Parades consisted of physical training & ceremonial whilst numerous football matches mainly against other teams in the Brigade group were indulged in the afternoon.'

I had to find the Forces canteen which was about eight miles away. It was in the centre of the 17th Division. Tom and Bill had put our stock in two big old biscuit boxes with tins full of all sorts of stuff that could keep well. We soon got going when Colonel Torrens said to me, 'I want to spend our profits on a Christmas dinner, Gregson, for the Battalion. So, just get in what you think we will want.' He said it was to be pork for our Brigade. I told him the Forces canteen allowed twelve dozen beers for each unit when they bought in.

He said, 'Stock up for a bottle each. It's Christmas dinner, 800 bottles would do.'

There were a lot of tee-total and dash men and I was one. We got 144 bottles that 6th December so by the time Christmas was at hand, we had enough. It was always Worthingtons Pale Ale which was twice as strong as French Ale.

Our canteen was at the village end as we had marched in. B Company quarters were in the school rooms and they were clean and we had toilets! The canteen had been lent by the farmhouse lady. She had a small boy Emile, 6, and two daughters, Marie, 10, and Sophia, 14. There was also an elderly farm hand, Marcel, who I would become very fond of. A happy Company helped us to clear farm things out of the outhouse and cleaned up. Tom and Bill made it comfortable to live there. We sold out of the window, all stocks from indoors. The boys came and got what they wanted.

Tom said, 'Sergeant, you will be going every two days.'

'Why?' I said.

'The boys are overspending. They're buying butter, tins, double biscuits, cake to be cut in larger sizes, cigarettes, cigars, candles, matches and spearmint – all are going very fast.'

They were actually buying it for the village.

I told the Colonel when I called next day for more money and he smiled, saying, 'As usual.'

'Well, it will keep you off parade and all the better for our Christmas Party.' He told me to keep quiet about the extras.

Christmas came.

The War Diary recorded Christmas Day thus, *'A football match in the morning between the Probables & the Possibles was followed by the Christmas dinners at 13:00 hours. These were a great success, the Acting Brigadier-General Lieutenant-Colonel G.L. Torrens DSO paying a welcome visit. The Officers of the Battalion dined together at 20:00 hours.'*

The B Company officers, Company Sergeant Major, Sergeants and Corporals were looking after the platoons. Twelve local French women cooked, dished it up and the Non-Commissioned Officers put it out for the troops. There was pork, sprouts, French beans, apple sauce and bottles of H.P. Sauce and Tomato Sauce. The Pale Ale was in bottles as we could not supply glasses so they drank it from the bottle. There were some cups belonging to the school but not many. The Christmas pudding was set on fire with rum and there was also sauce. Cigarettes and tobacco were also on the tables. Chocolate was given to those not wanting beer.

Each Company looked after itself. C Company was in the Church Hall, A Company was on an estate and D Company was in the school hall of the next village about 2 miles away.

We had all day to enjoy it. So our B Company danced old time. About 24 French women and some daughters, including our farmhouse mother with Sophia and Maria, joined us. The young ones danced with some of our young Tommies. They sang and danced and played games.

For tea, we had salad fresh from the farm with more pork and apple sauce, salad cream, bread and butter, strawberry jam and Christmas cakes.

At 7pm, we were just starting with our piano player playing our Regimental March, 'The British Grenadiers.' Our HQ Staff came in and Lieutenant-Colonel Torrens asked the boys if they were enjoying themselves. He said it was four years since the Battalion had Christmas Day out of the trenches. He spoke of achievements. Our old Colonel Wade was now Brigadier Wade. Lieutenant-Colonel Torrens said that Brigadier Wade sent his wishes, 'Hoping all have a good Christmas and he would be with his old Battalion, the 10th, in his thoughts.'

Before Lieutenant-Colonel Torrens, Major Thaker, Captain Forwood, Captain Smith, the doctor, and Captain Milne (Adjutant) and Captain Fryer went, the Lieutenant-Colonel added, 'I must mention to you, Sergeant Gregson. We have a reason to thank him, not only for thrilling us on a few occasions and winning our bets but he has worked hard since taking over our canteen, losing nights' rest and away early scouring the area to get you everything. You even asked for tripe and vinegar. Above all, we sold at cost, thanks to him – he wouldn't be happy selling for profit like other canteens. So, your old Commanding Officer Wade told him to have a free hand. The results are today's celebrations.'

Now Jack Hague and Drummy had a good time and the young boys and French girls gave Drummy tit-bits. Jack was a favourite when dancing with the ladies. He was awkward but willing and they roared at his French, 'Tray Bon, Wee Wee' which was about his limit. But language did not matter. We sang, danced and played games.

It began to thin out. The beer 'walers' went out to the estaminets.

I helped to wash up and pack up the articles borrowed mostly from the French. It was as good as over when the musicians went out. At 10.30pm, it was over and I thanked the helpers.

Our officers only came at dinner and tea times to see if all was going to plan.

I went home with our farmhouse family. Drummy went with Jack. He had a chain with a collar so Drummy came along and they put him in a kennel and fastened him in. Tom and Bill were also in the farmhouse.

'Vin Blanc et Vin Rouge,' the farm hands were going out for whatever they wanted. The girls retired after hot milk and kissing all when we went to our billets. Jack stopped with Tom and Bill and they opened a tin of (yes, you have guessed!) tripe with salt, pepper, vinegar, bread and butter. At 1am, we all settled down to sleep.

After we had such a good Christmas in 1918, New Year was now only one more day off.

I was at the British Expeditionary Forces canteen, buying in and the canteen Sergeant was doing his best to sell half a pig. He couldn't have liked our lads grunting! We had looked at it twice on the same day. I told him, 'I wouldn't know what to do with just half. It wouldn't be dripping butties for a Battalion.'

'No, Sergeant, you could sell it to the French.'

'That's more than I dare do,' I replied.

Well, I collected my stuff and Bob Bateman, the driver, took me back after the mules had taken off back to their stable.

Bob helped to pack the limber. The storeman, with the canteen Sergeant, came out with that half a pig cut right down from head to the tail, 'Pull your seat up, Lancs.'

I said, 'Take it off! I don't know what to do with it.'

He replied, 'Neither do I but away with it.'

Bob Bateman was a Colne youth, like Danny Hodson and Billy Hale from Gallipoli, and he said, 'Get it cut by D Company on our way and give their cooks first option of a share.'

We did just that and the cooks thought it was smashing.

Company Sergeant Major Moody, Sergeant Heitman and one or two cooks cut it into five parts for the Companies. Cheeky Charlie Hales was ticked off. 'Half a pig! What happened to t'other half? Run away!'

I'm not joking, Charlie and Bob Martin, his Wigan chum and fellow cook, were real comics, full of wit.

When I got to our canteen, I told Tom I had some pork. I was thinking of giving a party night if I could get Madame to cook the piece of pork.

Bill asked Marcel, the handy man, who said, 'Tres Bon,' so I went up to the farmhouse and I asked Madame. She was delighted to help me. On paper, she wrote 'Veg, sprouts or cabbage, cauliflower, roast potatoes or boiled and mashed, sauce.' So, it was settled. She cooked enough for nine. Five from the farm plus Tom, Bill and myself but, now, I was in the dark. Who was the ninth?

The children played with me, guessing who the ninth person would be. I said all sorts.

Have I spoken to him? 'No'

'Have I seen him?' 'No.'

'Has he seen us?' 'No, not yet.' 'Bientot.'

I soon understood all right as one child ended the guessing. 'Papa' came home at 4am this morning. He was demobbed from the Infantry. We would have a very good meal to celebrate.

With the remainder of the food, I asked Sergeant Swash to do what he liked. He wanted to pay me but I said, 'No.'

We had to go in at 6.30pm for 7pm dinner. Bill did all he could and took in biscuits, cake, cigarettes, cigars, matches, chocolate, spearmint, fruit, carnation milk and Three Nuns tobacco.

Marcel told Tom that 'his boss' would take some cigarettes with the meal, he liked strong ones. Sergeant Swash had given me a dozen pale ales. The girls got lemonade from the cafe.

Well, at 6.30pm, we got introduced to Papa. He wasn't what I expected. About my size and build, as I was then, and a bit more hair. He was a happy, kind man. A good family man with the three children climbing up on his knee and the boy climbing up the back of the chair with his arms round his dad.

He hadn't known much as he was just six years old and his dad had been away for about four years with perhaps a leave or two between August 1916 and New Year's Day January 1st 1919. So, he made a fuss of his dad. I am sure they had always told him about his dad.

We got polished up, shaved and washed for dinner. Madame placed us. I wanted to help carry the hot plates from off the stove. But 'No, No, the Ladies,' said Madame.

Dad, Tom, Bill and I were on one side then it was the boy next to dad, the two girls and, finally, Marcel, the handyman.

We started with a French grace for food and the sign of the cross. 'Bless us oh Lord, these thy gifts which we are going to receive from thy bounty through Christ our Lord Amen.' I know it off by heart now! It is the same today as it was in January 1919.

We tidied up, had biscuits and coffee (which was hand ground). We talked the best we could to the girls who knew a lot of 'soldier-talk' English such as 'Good Morning', 'Ow Do', 'Very Good', 'Eggs' and 'Cigs.' We sang some of our songs. Tom liked hymns and he had a fairly good tenor voice. Bill and I helped out the farmer with some French marching songs and he was good.

We had twelve bottles with glasses out on the table. Bill jumped up and stated, 'Another little drink wouldn't do us any harm.'

Tom and I followed him round the table then handed a bottle to them. Madame said, 'No, I don't want one' so four got opened.

Dad and Marcel said, 'strong, good', it was about three times stronger than their beer. I opened a bottle and got Sophia to bring a jug and two bottles of lemonade. I mixed pale ale with them and poured out a drop in three glasses and asked Madame to try.

Dad tasted it and then encouraged his wife to try some. She sipped at it then commented, 'Tres Bon, nice and cold.' She said they wanted more and she and dad wanted to know the name. I said in England it had two or three names. In the North, Centre, South East and West, the names I knew were shandy and 'a dash' of beer and pop lemonade mixed. He understood.

When Bill jumped up next time, they all got up and started going round. 'Another little drink,' said Bill which started them off.

'Drink!' Marcel shouted. It was fun but it finished the other six bottles. I asked Marcel to bring some from the estaminet.

'No,' Dad said, 'no, bon.'

We broke up about 10pm after a Christmas and New Year better than we had ever dreamed of.

I settled up with Madame the next day but it was Papa's celebration and she said it was God's doing. 'It had to be' just on dad's home-coming, 'even the pig was given for us.'

'Sergeant, we jamais forget never January 1st 1919. Never, every year Sergeant Gregson L.F.'s party.'

I often look back on that day, on other New Year's Day occasions.

It's been a while since the last run

It was the second week of January now and it was all about parade with lots of spit and polish.

On Saturday at mid-day, a runner from HQ came with orders to turn out for a cross-country run from the village pond at 3pm. I thought it was silly to run in such weather as it was freezing hard and we were doing cross-country in our boots. I got there and was told by C Company's Captain that it will be seven miles. I asked about other runners but 'only C Company,' was the answer. He started the race just as if it was a proper, competitive race, 'Ready, Steady, Go.' There were twelve with me, three C Company officers and nine others.

We had gone about half way when I asked one of the boys, 'You have been out before?' 'Yes, Sergeant, six times on this course.' I could tell that the flags on three feet high poles were already fixtures on the course.

I said, 'Come on, let's catch up with your officers.'

'I can't go any faster, we are running fast today.'

I caught a Lieutenant who said, 'Sergeant, I am going back, I am feeling sick.' I told him to take a cut across towards the church as it was a short cut. Then, when I reached Lieutenant Knight, he said, 'I was wondering where you had got to.' I told him that a Lieutenant had cut back feeling sick. 'Yes, I am not surprised, it's hospital for him. Can you catch Lieutenant Chalmers?'

'I don't know, he is well ahead,' but I tried. I got 20 yards behind just by the canteen when he shouted, 'Can't you stick it out?' I sprinted that last 100 yards to lead by at least ten yards. Captain Gale, who started us, was shouting that, 'It had been a trial.' I had been used as a trial horse.

At night, I met Colonel Torrens at HQ and was asked to go to Sergeant Swash, who told me to sit down. They were at C Company mess, so I had dinner first. When they had finished theirs, Colonel Torrens told Sergeant Swash he wanted to see me, so I went in.

'Now Sergeant, what happened this afternoon?'

'You ordered me to run, Sir, against my better judgement. I said it wasn't fit to race in. We could easily have got hurt, twisted an ankle, even broken a limb.'

'I suppose you are right, Sergeant. We have been to C Company HQ mess and Lieutenant Chalmers said he had you beaten and you would have packed in if he hadn't shouted to you that you couldn't stick it. Is that right?'

'Yes, Sir.'

'He must be good, don't you think?'

'Yes, Sir.'

I remember saying, 'Will someone tell me, firstly, why I was told to turn out? Secondly, why only C Company? And thirdly, why only me out of our other companies. Even Private Sammy Potter from C Company, the once 10th Battalion seven-mile cross-country champion, didn't turn out. Why?'

'It was Captain Milne our adjutant,' he said.

'Lieutenant Chalmers is our Battalion Sports Officer, Sergeant. Before Christmas, he was at a 17th Divisional sports meeting and got to know that the 17th Division would hold a seven-mile cross-country championship soon after the New Year. So, he thought we should be prepared for it.'

I said it would have been better to have had it put in our daily orders. 'He couldn't do that, we hadn't officially been told a race was taking place.'

'That's all right, Sir' I said. 'Do you know C Company have been out and have done today's run six times, just C Company. Our Battalion should have some other lads interested.'

We talked on until Colonel Torrens said, 'Lieutenant Chalmers is confident he will beat the Sergeant.'

'Well, I am not concerned in what he thinks, Sir. It is you saying he is confident he will beat me in that 17th Divisional race. Can I speak my mind, Sir?'

Major Forwood said 'Let him, Colonel, by all means, go on Gregson.'

I had to pause for coffee when Swash brought it in.

'To my mind, Sir, that run will take place soon.'

'What makes you say so?'

'C Company is being trained for it with a stray thrown in from B Company. They've done six cross-country runs round that course which is marked out with flags permanently placed. I should like to know why Private Sam Potter was not ordered to run, Sir. Just one more remark, Sir. Would you like to make a match with Lieutenant Chalmers, seven miles next Saturday round the same course? Battalion run, if you like, but the winner of me and the Lieutenant takes the bet.'

I left them, after asking them to let me know the date as soon as they got official word. I told Milne I wanted to know as soon as possible because I want to enter as an individual. C Company intended to run in it as a team for the team prize. I wanted to beat Lieutenant Chalmers. I told them that, in my spare time, I am going to get fit. No one had helped me up to then but if anyone wanted to accompany me on runs, they could and if anyone fancied the Lieutenant to win, 'let me have their bets.'

I left the six of them in laughter. Perhaps they had been pulling my leg and wanted to hear what I had to say.

It was that remark, 'Can't you stick it?' He had nothing to say at the start. He could have said, 'I want to run a trial, Sergeant, would you mind helping us out' or something like that but Captain Gale started us by counting seconds as if it was proper race.

Well, I did get down to it. Going for walks and runs when I was buying in. I would trot behind the cart or the limber. I would run and then walk with the mules. I was getting some good exercise. Three times in seven days, I went round that course. No one volunteered to come along with me.

The Adjutant sent word that the race was to take place on January 31st.

Two more weeks passed and I was helped by Marcel, the farm handyman. He had warm water ready for a wash down, a shower from a watering can and a hard towel rub after. He was excited and couldn't do enough. The two young daughters looked after my running clothes, washing and ironing. My rig out was the Warrington Athletic Club colours which were red with the 'Warrington' coat of arms on a sewn-on badge. This time, a white star was the coat of arms in the centre. The pants were white with inch-wide black tape sewn on each side, the length of the legs were twelve to sixteen inches long. A very nice turn out.

I was well looked after. Each time I ran out, the youths of the village ran with me as best they could. I had to go 300 yards down the main road, past the pond to reach the field. We had to get into the start. I say 'we', I mean myself. C Company stood aloft. What tickled me was when Captain Fryer called to see me and he told me that it had been arranged that I ran as a C Company Sergeant representing both C Company and the 10th Battalion Lancashire Fusiliers. He said no other Company had entered enough men to form a team of twelve with ten to count.

Every runner wore his numbers on the vest and the officials jotted down your number as you passed a two-mile post. At the three, four, five and six-mile markers, other officials did the same so a runner couldn't cut in somewhere.

The runner who came in first wouldn't receive his prize until all the officials had checked him in past the post and at the finish.

Now, the whole village was agog with excitement. It had got out that a Lieutenant and a Sergeant were racing. They knew something was to take place because C Company had been training for six weeks.

Our Marcel knew what, where and when. Tom and Bill told him to back Sergeant Gregson to beat C Company Lieutenant Chalmers with the C Company's backer. Bets were being placed in the Sergeants' mess or in the cafe, each night running up to the race.

Sergeant Heitman with his Crown and Anchor cards was taking bets. Jack bet 'evens' for Sergeant Gregson to beat Chalmers. Not to win the race but to beat the Lieutenant.

Thursday evening before the race and just after tea, I strolled round to the hairdressers with Dick (Private Richard Poole), the Catholic Priest's batman. I saw a pair of boots under a two-seater stool so, when he had finished, I went and picked them up. They were officer's boots. The hairdresser said I could have them if they fitted. He had got them off an Aussie officer who had a shave, hair-cut and then left the boots to be used or given away. I tried them on and they fitted like a glove.

'How much?' I asked.

'Nothing, Sergeant '

I said, 'Look, I am going to run on Saturday in them. They are a bit lighter than our boots.' All officers' boots had, in our Battalion at any rate, hob nails in and heel tips. I tried the boots on our farmer's fields and I was pleased. I don't think I was taking advantage of the others in the race. It was the 17th Divisional race, called a Championship, and everyone was to be in boots with a vest and pants to represent his unit.

So, all officers would be in their light boots, scores of them so I wasn't going to run against our C Company Lieutenant at a disadvantage, why should I? We were out to beat each other.

I got Marcel to black lead the bottoms of those boots, the shank mostly. So, if it was wet and sticky, it wouldn't stick for long. I wasn't taking any chances.

On Saturday morning, four motors were at the disposal of the Battalion to take all who wanted to go to Chaulette, 10 miles away. Our canteen lads Tom and Bill went with our farmer and his wife and family and my Marcel, all dressed up for the first time since 1914, a first day excursion.

In the farm there was a long cart with two horses. We had to be at the Company Sergeants' mess and cafe and I saw them going by. Red and white paper streamers and linen rosettes. I told Tom to put ten francs on for Mr and Mme and Marcel.

A C Company Sergeant was so sure of their Lieutenant beating me that they were getting their dinner ready at one o clock. Two large tables with white linen, glasses etc. for 7pm start.

When I got to their mess in the cafe, Company Sergeant Major Silcock invited me to their celebration after the race. I said that I would. When I got outside, our motors were filling up with fourteen runners. The motors got filled with the youngest children with their parents seeing them climbing up and in. I was their favourite if the red and white rosettes were anything to go by. I couldn't tell what they were saying, it was too quick.

We arrived safely one hour before the start. I went with Tom and Bill and watched the bets being placed. There was quite a queue and there were plenty of white colours from the C Company Lancashire Fusiliers soldiers.

I spent some time with Sergeant Swash, Sergeant Jack Heitman, Sergeant Harold Nolan, Private Jack Hague (but no Drummy) and the barber, just to pass the time before the race.

I went to our motor to get stripped off.

Remember, I was running as part of C Company. On the programme, our C Company was drawn as the second team. It was a good draw and it meant the No. 1 team were the Engineers and No. 2 was 10th Battalion Lancashire Fusiliers C Company.

So, our twelve runners were numbered 13 to 24. Our Lieutenant Chalmers was No. 13. I was No. 16 and a card was pinned on our vest back and front with big safety pins.

We were told to run straight down the long field passing the flags and keeping them always on our left and then round the haystack to the left. The 17th Divisional General, with a pistol ready, was just to our right on horseback. When we all reported present, he fired and off we went.

I shot off so I wasn't left in the ruck. 400 yards down to the haystack, I took the lead just as I turned left but was then obstructed by a big, Alsatian dog that leapt across at my back and over my legs. I was knocked over but there was just a scratch on my calf. I picked myself up just as the General (cracking his whip) shouted, 'Heel, heel! Are you alright? Who are you?'

'Sergeant Gregson, Lancashire Fusiliers, Sir.' I went on and saw twenty or more runners further on. They weren't grouped; they were stretched over about 50 yards or more in a single line so I hadn't much trouble in passing them. It meant going faster to get up to them which I did.

A Captain of the Engineers, No. 9, was leading with No. 13, Chalmers and No. 16, me, third.

We got to two signallers waving their flags at the entrance into a big wood and a path about two yards wide. They shouted, 'Take a ticket!' Moving out of the centre of the path, we had to get over a large uprooted tree. I had now taken the lead. I jumped on to the trunk, looked back and 20 yards behind was the Captain and our Chalmers, both neck and neck.

We got out of the woods and the Sergeants gave me a card with '1st Past' on it for when we handed them in at the finish, a further 800 yards up.

By that haystack to the roped off finish, it was like a 'V' shape. It went into a yard wide lane and we had to stop in our positions until our ticket, number, name, rank, and unit were taken.

First to finish was No. 16 Sergeant. G. A. Gregson, C Company, 10th Battalion, Lancashire Fusiliers.

I never enquired into our 10th Lancashire Fusiliers team numbers. C Company did not interest me then. I knew our lads stood a chance if all ten of us had finished the course.

We had first and second (Lieutenant Chalmers) and together that was three points only. All positions added so our other lads must have finished and ran well as we had won as a team, also.

The War Diary recorded on 31st January 1919, *'17th Division cross-country Championship was held at Hallencourt. This was won by the Battalion who also succeeded in getting the first two men home.*

Party of 1 Officer & 32 O.R.s left for demobilisation

Training throughout the period was confined mainly to physical drill & Education Class with various types of sports during the afternoon.'

I received two medals, the winners and a first team medal. These medals are now in the Archives at the Lancashire Fusiliers Museum in Bury.

Now you could imagine those lads of our old 4th Battalion Lancashire Fusiliers from Barrow, the two Jacks and Company Sergeant Major Moody from D Company and Hale Bank, Widnes, all won on the betting.

The French were kissing me and each other and our two girls, Sophia and Maria, and the young boy, Emile, were clinging to me excited and shouting to everybody. They knew the best surprise was the three to one Sergeant Gregson paid out at the stake. Tom handed 40 francs each to our farm owners. Marcel had also put his own on so he was all smiles although I didn't ask him how he fared.

Sergeant Jack had sorted out the bet for me; I won 300 francs plus 200 francs for first prize plus 30 francs that each team member got for the team prize. I gave the 30 francs to our two runners who couldn't take part, the eleventh and twelfth members of our team who were in reserve. It made them happy, fifteen francs each or about 10/2d in British money.

Well, it was all excitement. Captain Fryer had put his great coat on me as it was cold after I had been sweating. The Engineer Captain came to me, 'Well run' he announced and shook my hand.

'Well run, Captain. I am Sergeant Gregson, Sir.'

'I don't care who you are,' he said, 'you ran splendidly. The farther we went the more you left us, 200 yards or more after that dog incident. My name is Captain Greison of The Engineers. We have almost the same name but not the same speed.' I returned Captain Fryer's coat to him at Brigade HQ and then got to our motor. The others had gone on before we had got dressed.

The village was all in good humour. I couldn't get down from the motor before they smothered me, old and young. Company Sergeant Major Silcock rescued me, almost dragging me to C Company's mess. I got out the back way, to go down to the village to my billet with Tom and Bill. It was just the same there. The kiddies chanting and singing, marching and holding hands. We went to our HQ with a Brigadier and 3 cars of officers hooting, wanting to pass. I got the crowd to break loose for the Commanding Officer to get through. They all waved as they got clear.

I finally got cleaned up with the help of all. The French and Bill polished my buttons, badge and boots (my own this time!) and I shaved, washed and made myself presentable. Marcel had a shower ready when I entered the farm so that was a good start.

I had felt a kind of guilt when I returned into C Company's mess. They all lost on the betting. The officers and non-commissioned officers in the mess had all backed Lieutenant Chalmers – the man who had asked me, 'Can't you stick it, Sergeant?' He never even spoke to me at the finish. He was next to me waiting, but it was the Engineer's Captain who was interested.

We had a good dinner with free drinks with it. I was sent for at 8pm by the HQ mess. I was congratulated when the Brigadier spoke, he said, 'We have met, Sergeant?'

I said 'Yes, Sir. Contalmaison.'

'How did you leave Private Brindle?' Looking first in his note-book. I prompted him, 'The doctor told me he would be in Blighty that time the next day.'

The Brigadier said, 'He got to a northern hospital who said it would slightly alter his speech but he was really lucky.'

Grandpa, the soldier

Grandpa, the solider, standing with Jack Ratcliffe from Warrington and Harry Gardner from Nelson. Harry's father was Headmaster of the grammar school at Horwich and Grandpa later came across Harry in difficult circumstances at Gallipoli

Collecting stock for the canteen? Grandpa is the soldier on the right together with, possibly, Bob Bateman, Tom Chadwick from Rochdale and Bill Smith from Salford

Rue Saint-Louis, Hallencourt

Christmas card from the front, and right, inside the christmas card, mapping the path taken by the 17th Division, including the 10th Battalion Lancashire Fusiliers, between 17th August and 11th October 1918

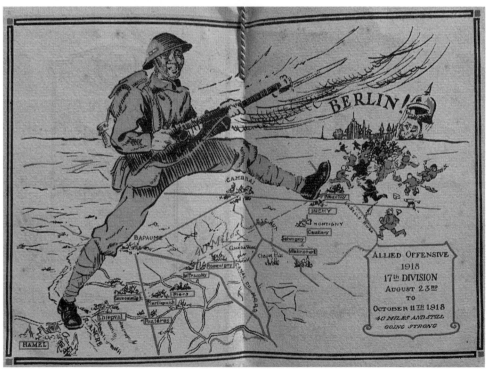

H.Q.,
55th Division.

No. 6159. Sgt. GREGSON, G.A.

The above mentioned N.C.O. is reporting in accordance with instructions received from 52nd Infantry Brigade (17th Div:)

He has been selected as a Member of the B.E.F. Cross-Country Team.

On completion of his duty with you will you please instruct him to return to the 4th Bn. The "Kings" (Liverpool) Regt - 33rd Division as he is now on the strength of that Unit.

Captain & Adjutant,
26-3-1919. 10th (S) Bn. THE LANCASHIRE FUSILIERS.

Grandpa was called back from leave in March 1919 to represent the British Expeditionary Forces in a Cross-Country race at Brussels

C O P Y.

Officer Commanding

&th. Bn. "The King's"(Liverpool Regt).

I beg to notify that the N.C.O. mentioned below has been selected to represent Troops in France & Flanders at the Army Athletic Championship Meeting at Aldershot on August 28th. & 29th., and to request that he may be permitted to remain at Calais for training purposes until the team crosses to the United Kingdom on August 25th.

SGT. GREGSON.

(Signed) G.S.BROWN.
Major.
Supt. Physical Training.
British Troops in France & Flanders.

Headquarters, P.T.
Wimereux.
9-8-19.

Grandpa was selected to represent the Troops in France and Flanders at the Army Championships at Aldershot in August 1919

The Team from France and Flanders at the Army Championships at Aldershot 1919. Grandpa is the first man on the left on the top row. Following a boat journey home and a significant bout of seasickness, Grandpa felt he'd not done 'too badly' finishing 4th

PART SIX

Staying on 1919

The Battalion starts to de-mob but its another twelve months for me

WELL, IT WAS OVER with another day worth remembering. It would take too long to write about all that took place. 500 francs about £17, not a bad day's pay and good entertainment.

On the 2nd February, the War Diary stated, *'The Battalion Cross-country team, having won the Divisional Competition, secured third place in the 5th Corps contest. Sergeant Gregson was second man home.'*

Soon after, our Battalion started demobbing.

Twenty, thirty going, weekly. Jack Hague was one of the first to go but Drummy wouldn't go. Jack Heitman had gone. As time went on, we had to pack up the canteen. January was gone and so had two weeks of February.

I became pals with Sergeant Bert Langdon from Blackpool. He was in our Battalion orderly room. I asked Bert when he thought he and I were going to get our papers. 'Greg,' he said 'the Adjo told me, we would be the last. We're not married, not even engaged.'

They knew something. Our Captain Milne did a lot of censoring of letters. I remember him coming along the front trench when he spotted me. 'Gregson, would you give this letter back to your Sergeant pal, Heitman? I don't know how you got matey with that kind of man. Tell him he ought to be ashamed of himself.' When I gave it to Jack, he said, 'the next one I write he won't get chance to read.'

Captain Milne will have known that I never wrote to a wife because I wasn't married, not even courting.

Sergeant Bert Langdon, a day or two after, said, 'I am going to sign on for twelve months more.' So, I did also and our Adjutant did the signing on part for us. On 18th February 1919 we signed on again, we'd not had enough!

Bert and I got fourteen days leave. After five days at home, a telegram came and asked me to return at once to the 55th Division HQ at Brussels to run for the Army. The message was from Captain Milne.

Well, as a true soldier I got straight back and I found eleven officers, non-commissioned officers and a Physical Training Sergeant there and they had been for eight days. We trained daily, both running and PT. On the following Sunday morning, we ran a ten-mile cross-country race against the Belgian Army. I finished third with a Captain from the Belgians first and Sergeant Wally Garside second. I was 150 yards behind the leader which was not too bad as it was ten miles without enough training. This time, it was the honour of representing the British Army.

I stayed two weeks, all told.

That afternoon after our race we all had free admission to a soccer game, the Belgium vs England match and our lads won 4 – 0.

I remember one player very well. He was a first-class cricketer as well as a footballer, JWHT Douglas. We knew him as 'Johnny Will Hit Today. J.W.H.T.D.'

Bert and I had been assigned to the 4th Battalion King's Liverpool Regiment. I was still in Brussels when Bert asked Major Brown to find out where the Regiment was stationed. It was no use, no one knew anything and he gave up four days later. Eventually, Major Brown gave me orders to report to Etaples on the west coast of France. I was busy weighing up my movement order.

I left Brussels on the 9th March 1919 for Etaples. Firstly though, I wanted to do some visiting.

I got off at the station five miles from Caudry. I showed the Station Master my movement order. He could read English but didn't care either. The war was finished, that was all I could understand from him.

When I got to Vergies, only Madame, of the family I spent New Year with, was at home. She was pleased to see me. She apologised for not having something for lunch. I asked her if I could stay for a week or so. 'Yes, you are welcome.'

I told her I had won with running and betting and I showed her my two 17th Divisional medals, she was glad I had done so well.

I gave her five twenty-franc notes to buy in with and paid 30 francs per day. She went out.

I found a pen and ink and did what I had wanted to do ever since

I studied my movement order. I had left on the 9th and just put a one with the 9th and it made 19th March. It was in figures not writing so no one would doubt it. To my thinking, our new unit, the 4th Battalion King's, were lost on the move and I supposed then to tell the truth didn't matter.

I was welcome here so nothing mattered.

I went early Sunday morning after breakfast to Inchy Beaumont where Georgette and Isabelle's family were glad to see me again. They expected their dad and son home soon out of the Army. I wouldn't stay quietly; I spoke to Madame and gave her 50 francs to buy something good for Sunday dinner. After a while she took it. I didn't want to make it look like pity. I said, 'Take this and buy in for Sunday dinner and think of me when you have it.'

Two francs would buy some meat, potatoes, vegetables, pudding, coffee and bread for five. I promised that if it were possible for me to call again someday, then I would.

I made the same promise with the Caudry family where the dad was doing morning work for the 'Corporation', cleaning the road and general work. Naomi, the daughter, was still at the YMCA but they told her that if she could get work somewhere else she should take it, so that didn't sound too good.

Before I left on the morning of the 19th March for Etaples, I promised to get back to see them but never dreamt I would.

At Etaples, they put me in the Sergeants' mess. After enquiring about future movements, they said that nothing was known yet so I was told to go and get my bed ready for the night. I did two nights there and then was given movement orders on the 21st to move from Etaples to Harfleur near Le Havre. I reported in but nobody was interested, only Sergeant Berry and a group of men from the old 10th Battalion Lancashire Fusiliers' Battalion who, now, like me had been sent to the 4th King's Liverpool Regiment.

The War Diary records, '*163 men from the 10th Battalion Lancashire Fusiliers joining the Regiment on 29th March 1919.*'

What I saw didn't please me at first glance. The men were young and hadn't had much active service or, indeed, discipline. Our Lancs men could be picked out on parade. Sadly, the 4th King's Liverpool Regiment had suffered very heavy losses in the war and, particularly, in the Battle of the Somme.

The Regimental Sergeant Major 'Big Jim' was a real Liverpudlian Scouser, it would be better not to mention his name. He was ten years younger than me and had been rushed into being a Regimental Sergeant Major. 'You have come to a regiment of honoured fighting men,' he told me. Looking at him and some of the others, I didn't think of their honour and I wouldn't know about fighting, perhaps, street corner boys more by their looks and ways.

Big Jim had set himself against our old 10th Boys. He would come over to where Bert or I were drilling our platoons and giving them PT. He told us to, 'Give them ceremonial parade.' Believe me, they didn't know what 'ceremonial' meant, I'm sure the instruction was just to make me feel sore. It so happened that as Captain Nickels came along, I was fed up. Big Jim shouted, 'Shape yourself, Gregson.'

I saluted the Captain saying, 'The Regimental Sergeant Major blames me for most of the platoon not knowing what the ceremonial drill is. They've never done it. Let me pick my lads, they know it, Sir.'

'You do your best Sergeant. Teach them.'

Captain Nickels took the Regimental Sergeant Major away. I got eight old 10th lads who were in my platoon and put them through it. Then I told our boys to get in their places. Tallest on the right, shortest on the left. We got through it.

I told Company Sergeant Major Bird what the Regimental Sergeant Major had given me to do. He said, 'Well done, Gregson, I bet you got your platoon to do it. I will give our lot that tomorrow.'

Now Big Jim went too far one morning. Sergeant Bert was detailed for the main guard. He picked his own lads; eight of them had already cleaned the night before. They had washed and 'Blanco'd' equipment and polished their boots. When he got to HQ, the Lieutenant (no name) on duty and the orderly Sergeant and the Regimental Sergeant Major inspected Bert's guard. They were the worst Big Jim had ever inspected apparently. 'Go back! I give you an hour to return something like soldiers,' the Lieutenant said.

Now that was where Big Jim dropped a clanger. Half-way back to his hut a Brigadier with his Aide de Campe were coming towards Bert who gave 'Attention Eyes Left' and saluted. If anyone knows Harfleur, it was at the 'pimple', running alongside the road.

The Brigadier stopped the guard and wanted to know where they were going. He had never met a guard going that way at 9.30am. Bert told him what the Regimental Sergeant Major said.

The Brigadier replied, 'Sergeant, march them back, I will inspect your guard.' When Bert got back, all were there, the Commanding Officer, the Adjutant, the Orderly Sergeant Officer and the Regimental Sergeant Major. The Brigadier was talking all the while about what he liked. The packs, for instance, as no boards were needed to make them square. The men were neat and square without them.

'In future, tell your guards not to use wood of any kind. Excellent.'

He asked the Colonel to look down one of the lad's rifles.

'You know,' he said, after he had finished his inspection and standing in front of Bert, 'you know, these boys belong to the Twentieth of Foot, not to the King's Liverpool. Did you know Sergeant Major they still put the double cross in their puttees? You must take it out now; it should be just plain without two crosses.'

We used to put them on as instructed on our Lancashire Fusilier service. We liked to twist our puttees as it looked as if they would never come loose, which they did at times. Big Jim had missed it but the Brigadier hadn't. The laugh was with Bert and his old Lancashire's squad.

That night, all was in order. They were a guard to be proud of. They were clean, sharp and marching like the 'Guards do' with heads up and packs neat and square. Congratulations to Brigadier so and so. The men were also signed off by our Adjutant Captain Dawson of the 4th King's Liverpool.

Bert told Company Sergeant Dicky Bird and me all about it. 'You can knock spots off our lot. But we have not always been like this, Bert,' Dicky said, 'our best are home by now.'

'Yes, Sergeant Major' Bert said, 'my boys are just like yours, not got enough service in to be demobbed.'

Bert was pleased when he knew the Brigadier had praised the 4th Battalion King's Liverpool's guard as a real 4th Battalion of the King's Liverpool Regiment.

The next day, Big Jim had another go at me in the Sergeants' mess. 'Have you learnt the ceremonial parade yet, Gregson?'

It was always 'Gregson' from him and I didn't like it.

'Yes, Jim'

'Sir!' he shouted.

Quietly, I said, 'say Sergeant Gregson and then I will respect your rank.' Remember, this was taking place in our Sergeants' mess, not on parade. So, in the mess, the Sergeant was in charge, it was their mess rules.

The Regimental Sergeant Major tried to provoke me. I told him, 'Next time, tell me to teach them from the start because if you had taught that the first order was to fall in with the tallest on the right, they surely could have shaped better. Your Captain Nickels told me to be patient with them and asked me to teach them two or three other things that the men hadn't been taught yet.'

'Such as what Sergeant Gregson?' he replied.

'Well, Sir, it's evident you haven't read tonight's orders. I have 30 minutes on how to pack a soldier's kit and place it in a knapsack so as to make it square without using boards.'

He responded, 'You belong to the 4th King's Liverpool and don't forget it.' 'No, Sir, I won't,' I replied.

It was time for other pre-occupations!

Our Captain Doctor saved me just at that moment when a message came. It read, 'Sergeant Gregson, I should like five minutes talk if you would kindly call at our HQ mess at 5pm tonight?' It was nearly that. By now, Bird and I were playing draughts so I told Bird I would play with him again later.

When I got to the mess, the Doctor told me I had a staunch supporter, a Lance Corporal Moss. 'One of our old 10th Lancashire Fusiliers, Sir' I replied.

The Doctor continued, 'I was treating Lance Corporal Moss, when I asked him if he had brought any athletes with him from the 10ths. He had said, 'Yes, one, a Sergeant, you haven't any in this mob to beat him from one mile to 10 miles.

I asked him if Moss was very sick, 'Nothing that I cannot cure' was the answer. 'Two days off with medicine will put him back again. Now, we are holding a Battalion Sports up on the pimple top on Saturday and I will watch you. I am the Sports Officer and I represent the 4th

King's Liverpools on the General Committee and the Committee have decided to hold a France and Flanders Sports Championship in the near future. So, I have arranged a sports day to see if we had any lads fit to represent our unit.'

The War Diary reports, *'Battalion Sports on 17th May 1919.'*

The doctor had played association football for Hoylake before the war. He could sprint a bit but did not do long distance. I asked him if the Regiment had any milers, 'No, our best have gone,' he said. 'You will see our best on Saturday, a poor lot I am afraid. I will be interested watching you.'

'Will there be any betting?'

'I can't say. The Company officers of each company might back their men.'

'I should like to have a bet on to make me try,' I said.

'What are the prizes?' I asked.

'£2, £1 and 10 shillings only for the principal events, the 100, 220, and 440, half-mile and mile. The other events are the comical ones for whoever wants to have fun, like the three-legged wheelbarrow race. It will be on Saturday from 2.30pm till 4.30pm on the parade ground of the Engineers. It will be measured and marked by them. They seem older soldiers but good natured.'

I went up on Tuesday and Thursday at 3pm to do a bit although it was too late to do a lot of heavy training. It would make one stiff and sore for Saturday and it would be better to run without soreness. That would come on the Sunday and Monday after the sports!

Well, those Engineers got quite pally. They were keen and they said, 'It will be you, Sergeant that we will back on Saturday.'

Well, to cut it short it doesn't need a running commentary. It was a classic Sports Day. I sent a note to the Doctor that said I would enter the 880 yards and one mile. If they had a relay race, which was not mentioned on the form, I would do the 440 or 880 yards for my B Company.

I easily won the 880 yards and the mile and I had a bit of fun being the wheelbarrow in the event with Sergeant Jackson holding my legs up as shafts. We were second. I won the 40 yards blind race. Those prizes were all sorts stuffed into a linen bag including razors and blades, a tooth brush, Colgate toothpaste and writing pads plus £4 for what was, in reality, a nice day of training.

Company Sergeant Major Bird said the relay fell through as, 'Sergeant Gregson, with the 880 yards running last, would lick anyone of their runners, it would be hopeless.' I didn't mind it was just nice to start training for the big event that the doctor had mentioned.

I went out on Monday afternoon to loosen up, doing what I thought was necessary. I was training for the mile. I always judged the mile my best, although I did the 880 yards once at Warrington Sports in 1 minute 56 seconds. It was the winning time on the board and won a large £7 7 shillings case of cutlery which eventually became a present for Bernard, my son, and John and Martin, my grandsons.

Those old soldiers were quite enthusiastic, I got to like them.

Sergeant Scott, a fine man, wanted to look after me but I told him one man, a Lance Corporal was already doing just that.

They got bits of bets on the Saturday Sports, just for 'bacci' as one Irishman said.

Now, I got detailed for guard duty at Bethune Railway Station. Placing three men and a non-commissioned officer in charge when the train came in at Bethune, we replaced the guard who had brought it up from the base. We took the train to the next relief near the Belgium border and then we returned by the passenger train to our camp, just next to the station.

I didn't know who picked me for it but it turned out just what the doctor ordered!

Lieutenant Delmer was supposed to be in charge but he left it all to me. There were fourteen all told in that camp. The Lieutenant, one Sergeant, one Corporal, two Lance Corporals and nine Privates plus a batman who was one of the Privates who cooked for us. The batman also looked after Lieutenant Delmer.

I was out on the roads doing a bit of distance running to take a bit of surplus off and get down to nine stone or eight stone twelve pounds, my lowest then.

Mr Carpentier, who lived directly opposite our camp billet, asked me why I was running. He had been an athlete, French, running long distance races. He told me to run on the Artillery Training Ground that was 300 yards down the road which I did.

I asked an officer on parade if I could use the centre to run round and he said, 'Avec plaisir'. It was only a small grass circuit.

There was a big enclosure with cindered earth for the horses with gun carriages. In 1914, there were not many motors, they came later.

I used to run about twenty laps and then dash back to camp.

Lance Corporal Ginger Moss (the old 10th Lancashire Fusilier soldier) prepared a bath in a large tin barrel with fairly hot water and plenty of soap. The best was his old petrol tin with nail holes punched in the bottom. He had fastened it up by nailing it to a post. I stood under it and he mounted some bricks and poured warm water in the petrol tin and I got a shower that way. It was fun as well as doing me good. It took place in our camp ground in a broken down out-house which had been bombed or hit with a shell.

I was feeling good when our Captain Nickels came to visit the camp at Bethune and examined all the duties we had done and who had done them. He said, 'I see you went on one guard. Why Sergeant?'

'Because I was the only NCO available on that afternoon, the other two guards hadn't returned so I took the remaining two Privates and carried on, Sir.'

He handed me a sealed letter marked 'Private, Sergeant Gregson'. It was from the doctor. 'You are entered for the Mile Race and it takes place at Bethune ('you lucky blighter, Sergeant!'): Sports Committee, 1:30pm till 5 pm at the Artillery ground on Saturday 10th June 1919.'

It was ten days off as it was then the end of May and the weather was at its best.

Warm and sunny in the evening, I went fishing with Mr Carpentier in the Bethune canal. It was relaxing and quiet. We made ourselves understandable to each other – 'peche' is fishing? We became good friends. I was lucky that way, I always had pals.

Mrs Carpentier washed my clothes, including the running things. I sharpened my spikes as it was better for me, sharp in and sharp out.

Two days before the race, Bethune began to get excited. I went to the hairdresser just up the road. He asked if I would win the race and which race was I in. He wanted to back me. I told him, 'The one-mile at 3.30pm,' and he copied it down. He had noticed me training, going past to the sports field. He had two more customers in the cafe and they wished me luck on Saturday. The barber said he was going to the sports meeting to bet and have a good time. Not since before 'la guerre', had they rejoiced. So, now, he said he will put his flag out which I saw him do. That started others doing the same.

On Friday night, Lance Corporal Ginger Moss came back to camp at about 8pm. 'Sergeant, do you want a bet? I took on a RAMC Sergeant. He is spending his leave knocking about France. He is in lodgings by a cafe in the next street. He laid me three to one to name the winner of the mile. Why the mile? I asked him and he replied, 'Because our officer is a good thing.' Ginger continued, 'I put all I had on, twenty francs, and told him to wait as I would go and get more. The Sergeant had asked him, 'Who is your man?' and I replied, 'Sergeant G. A. Gregson, the 4th Battalion King's Liverpool.' Ginger said the Sergeant had taken the bet, and handed over our 40 francs plus another 60 francs to the Madame of the cafe.'

The town on Saturday morning was filling up with soldiers from twenty miles around. The estaminets and cafes were doing a good trade and Mr and Mme Carpentier were busy. She found time to do my washing.

I ran in spikes and I had my numbers sent to me for the one-mile only. It said 'G.A. Gregson 4th K.L'S Regiment No. 6.'

I gave Ginger Moss 50 Francs to put on.

Our Captain Doctor was with my Company Captain Nickels and Lieutenant Delmer. They went up after 2pm lunch to the Sports ground and were soon in the totalisation tent.

I appeared to be popular with the French artillery soldiers who had been seeing me in training on their ground. Also, the Bethune people were all dressed up and were out for excitement.

The barber waited by the runners' tent. 'You must victoire', well, it sounded like that to me.

3.30pm came and I was ready. There were 26 runners and I was No. 6.

The course was full of bends over seven laps with the bell being rung to start the seventh lap.

Bang! We were off. I did not want to be left and stuck in the ruck. Cutting out on bends was difficult and you were liable to get tripped or spiked. I was running second for the first three laps and I wasn't pushing so I stepped it up a bit and passed the stocky leader with four laps gone. On the fifth and sixth laps, I had a six yards lead when the bell went.

I hadn't waited for it to ring when I shot off then the French let themselves go. 'Sergeant, Sergeant, Sergeant bravo,' they were yelling, shouting and chanting. It was all encouragement and I won rather easily by 50 yards.

I was the only runner in red so I was easily picked out. About ten runners still had to run their last lap when I had finished. Now the Doctor first got to me at the finish.

'Well done, Sergeant,' he said.

I replied, 'That wasn't a mile',

'It was, you know' he replied.

'Can you ask for the time keeper? Ask for the time of the 3-mile which had been run at 2.30pm.'

The doctor came back. The three-miler had been won in ten minutes twenty seconds. I won the one-miler in 3 minutes 13 seconds, just around a minute faster than our English Champion in those days 1919! I could tell it was short and that was why I shot off before the bell for the last lap. It was 350 yards short of a mile, it was ridiculous.

To think our British Sports Committee should mark out a circle so small and not work it out, another four laps were needed. It should have been eleven laps, not seven! It was the same for all the twenty-six runners and no one had an advantage, all did seven laps and were off the same mark. The tote paid 'four to one Gregson' to my surprise. So, I wasn't the only one fancied. Captain Ollier of the Royal Army Medical Corps was 50 yards behind in second.

Ginger Moss picked up his money on his way back to camp. I won £5 or 140 francs for first prize and 200 francs off the tote for my 50-franc bet, about £6 10 shillings on the day.

Our camp did well. The barber and Mr Carpentier were kissing my cheek and giving me hugs. It was all strange but nice, they were happy and it had been a long time since they could let themselves go, it was overdue.

Lieutenant Delmer did well at the officer's club with bets. Mr Carpentier had 20 francs on so he won 80 francs profit. They were delighted. It was very nice to have been able to help out. I think, perhaps, the barber got the same four to one rates.

I took Friday night guard at 9pm. The train came into Bethune so it was 10pm when the driver and the French guard in his last van were ready for Belgium.

Another sad tale – Another Soldier doesn't return home

We got back to Arras and then got into the train to go back to Bethune.

There were three of us in a compartment by ourselves. A gent and a young lady got onboard just as the train started. They came along the corridor, looked in and saw we were soldiers then went on along the train. They came back and he put three cases on the luggage rack. She had a large cardboard box on her lap. We chatted and laughed, taking no notice.

She said, 'Sergeant, did I hear you mention Bethune?'

'You certainly did. We are in camp next door to the station, in a billet.'

'Would it be too much trouble for you to take my box to your billet? We are going to Lens, to the mines. We will call about 3pm for it.' I told her not to worry as I would personally take it and look after it.

She said, 'My brother is buried in a cemetery outside Bethune,' but she did not know exactly where. We got out at Bethune.

I told Lieutenant Delmer the box contained a cross for a Lieutenant Sisson. Bethune was on the label. Lieutenant Delmer got washed, shaved and changed. His batman was going dizzy cleaning Delmer's boots, buttons and badges and sponging his clothes off.

I got to know from Mr and Mme Carpentier where the main cemeteries were. 'Go past our fishing spot, first turn on the right, down the main road for 300 to 400 yards, down on the right,' was the instruction.

The lady and gent came and I got the box out to give to them. The gent (a Yankee) said, 'Put it inside.' They had chartered a French soldier's motor transport, two seats on the front row including the driver and three at the back. The lady asked if I would like to come. 'Yes, I will, if you don't mind.'

We went over the humped back bridge over the canal, turned left, passed, on our left, our fishing place along that canal road. The driver flew passed the first turn on the right. I shouted for the driver to stop and he did.

The Yank asked what the matter was. I said, 'It is down the road we have just passed,' but the driver said, 'We know where we are going.' So, I replied, I'll get out here and have a walk in that case.' They carried on and I trotted down that road on the right. There was a solitary soldier at the cemetery weeding and tidying up with a spade, rake and barrow. I spoke to him after I had got in and fastened the gate on the road side.

I told him a party of three were looking for a Lieutenant Sisson. 'I have one Sisson only, he could be it.'

'Do you know what unit he was in?' 'No, only the name.'

'Will you help me?'

'I will do,' he replied, 'you start at the top one in row 15.'

I found Sisson so I went up to the soldier's cabin and then washed and cleaned up the gravestone. The soldier carried on and I saw him clean and wash about twelve other gravestones around Sisson. Sisson's was the fourth down on the row so it didn't look as though it was done just for them. The soldier had nine hundred graves to look after.

I told him they were coming and he met them at the gate and took them to his cabin office. He took all the particulars; it was her brother's grave. We all went with the keeper to the grave. She placed the cross on it, knelt down in prayer with tears streaming down her face. I strolled on a bit when Lieutenant Delmer came. 'Why were you so sure you knew this place?'

'Mr Carpentier told me all soldiers killed in and around Bethune got buried there. They went to the first big service for the dead.'

The soldier thanked me for letting him know. He said she could see the graves were well looked after, she would probably call again before she returned home to England.

When we got back, she wouldn't have a cup of tea. She thanked me saying, 'You knew, Sergeant, where he was buried.'

'Mr and Mme Carpentier there at their cafe door had told me.' I replied. She looked across and waved to them. Mme Carpentier blew her a kiss. They went on their way and we went to tea.

We got relieved after six weeks of guard duty. We had to join up at Douai in a French barracks. The Battalion had moved there on 18th June 1919.

It was a big fine place with gardens in front with a bandstand. Our

4th King's Liverpool's band played on Tuesday, Thursday and Sunday at 7pm each night.

The French loved it. Each night, they clapped, cheered and shouted for them to play. 'We made a bonfire of our troubles'.

I was told to keep up my training. The doctor wanted me to get off parades. But I didn't want that. When on parade, your mind was on your next order and not moping about your next race.

Well, alongside all the old 10th Battalion Lancashire Fusiliers, who had signed up with the 4th King's Liverpool Regiment, a certain dog had also followed the same path. Drummy the dog was still with us! It was now Ginger Moss who mostly fed him.

It was strange; Drummy had been on a route march since 'signing' with this Regiment. Stray dogs came in the camp but he didn't bother with them, sleeping and meals were his only care.

Sergeant Graham was also his pal and I don't know why. I had been in the German trench when we found Drummy, I had been with him in the trenches, I had fed him water and found him food but he didn't show any signs of coming to me for a good walk. He was also a bit too heavy to run with me.

Well, I trained seriously running round the parade square and walking round the outskirts of Douai. I received a letter instructing me to race. I had to be at Valenciennes for Friday 22rd July at 4pm for a mile race. This was a qualifying race to represent the Douai area in the France and Flanders Championships to be held in August in Calais. If I did well at these Championships, I could represent France and Flanders at the Army Championships at Aldershot later in August.

My number enclosed in my letter for Valenciennes was No. 3. It was 170 francs for first, 85 francs for second and 40 francs for third. When I reached the Sergeants' mess, a Sergeant Reynolds from St. Helens was down for the 220 yards.

He said he felt like sleeping in a soft bed. 'Let's go into town and book a bed and breakfast room,' which we did.

We retired at 10.15pm to our beds. At 11pm, our room was all lit up from a fair, just at the back! There was an organ, a big loud one, and it was only in tune for half the time. It would occasionally stop for about a minute but it made a terrible noise. Stopping every now and then and then starting off again. And, it was just the one tune, 'The Last Waltz'. It was 2am when they eventually shut down. Reynolds got out of bed two or three times. I didn't, I tried my best to forget it but you couldn't. It was most annoying but one of those things one could not do anything to change.

For breakfast, they brought out two boiled eggs with bread, French cobs, butter and coffee. So, we didn't do so badly. I had been disturbed on other occasions all night, especially the five nights and days on the Somme in July 1918, twelve months earlier!

We had a light lunch in the Sergeants' mess then went up to the Sports Ground. I was getting ready for 4pm, my time to be out on the mark for the mile when Sergeant Reynolds came running. He said, 'I ran awful, fourth so I didn't qualify. You haven't much chance, Gregson.' He told me a South African named Corporal Schwartz, a six-footed blond, big-built soldier, was running. 'He has a big following, stationed with the Engineers in this area. I spoke to one of them and they have backed him on the tote.'

I got out 50 francs, they were large notes. I had never seen notes so large, they folded 4 times and were still then a lot bigger than our £1 note. I told him to put it on for me, now. He looked amazed. 'You haven't seen him,' he said. 'Never mind his looks, get that on please,' I replied. The odds will be good. I haven't anybody with me so I will scoop the odds.' He said, 'Ok, I will risk it too, twenty francs I'll bet Greg.' Later, he told me, 'There were no bets taken on you, Sergeant, only ours.' A Company Sergeant Major was backed as No.1. 'The Corporal is No. 9, you No. 6,' Reynolds told me.

We got the usual instructions. For the mile race, the bell will ring for the last lap of four. There were twenty runners with the first three to qualify to run at Calais in August. We were told this before we started.

We all dashed off. The big youth, with only short pants on and wearing spikes, had his number pinned to his shorts, No. 9. He took a lead of five yards, just in front of me but I was third when we finished that first lap. The Company Sergeant Major was No. 1, he ran in a red top with black pants. He looked a regular soldier with straight up shoulders and back bronzed. I went up to No. 9, the South African. He thought I was going to pass so he rushed on and kept at it. I didn't let him get too far ahead as we had two more laps to do.

He got anxious and spurted on. The bell rang and he was ten yards in front half-way round that last lap. I speeded up at a pace that I could stick at. He sprinted when I tried to pass, but I went all out then and beat him by ten yards. He collapsed after he passed the line.

Sergeant Reynolds was delighted. I won all right. The Brigadier said, 'You ran a tactical race, you had the Corporal worried all the while. Sergeant Gregson, you will run in the final on the 8th August.'

He shook hands and gave me a packet with 170 francs and a card saying, 'Winner Sergeant G. A. Gregson 4th Battalion King's Liverpool Regiment,' in ink which had just been written.

The tote paid six to one on the winner so not many had backed me.

Reynolds was pleased as he was 120 francs to the good. He said our boys will be annoyed as they could have come to the sports but they didn't think it was worth it. He did, just over £4 was good going.

For me, it was almost £6 winner's prize and 300 francs on the tote so, on the day, it was worth about £16 18 shillings. So, I thought it was worth it!

We used to sing 'Ho, Ho, Ho, it's a Lovely War!' And that seemed about right that day. Also, in the packet, there was a note, 'Please report on Monday for training' so I was off again.

Back at Douai, for just a week, it was mostly walking for me.

The doctor said it served him right for not going along with me to Valenciennes. I never got much of a following. The best support that I got was at the 17th Division seven-mile championship where the whole village and half the 10th Battalion Lancashire Fusiliers turned up.

In the Sergeants' mess, it was dull. Only Sergeant Jackson, Company Sergeant Major Bird, Sergeant Graham, Bert and Sergeant Wilson were very pleased with my win. Big Jim said, 'I see our Lancashire Fusilier, Sergeant Gregson, scraped through again.'

Now that was too much for Bert Langdon. 'Will our Regimental Sergeant Major like to have a bet as Sergeant Gregson of the King's Liverpool Regiment won't scrape through in the final next Friday?' Big Jim surrounded himself with his disciples, his 'yes and no, Sir' men. To them, the Regimental Sergeant Major was always right but Company Sergeant Major Bird always spoke his mind.

'We ought to be proud of our Sergeant. He is out miles on his own in our regiment, there's no one to give him a race and no one has helped him. He goes on and on and no one is encouraging him, only 'a scrape through' from his Regimental Sergeant Major.'

Big Jim said, 'You appear to lean to those old Lancashire Fusiliers.'

'No, I don't,' replied Bird, 'but I do like fair play. I give credit when I see it is needed. You must know those Lancs can be picked out easily amongst our lot. They're clean and smart and, above all, disciplined at all times on or off parade and I say good luck from me on the 8th at Calais.'

Sergeant Bert Langdon asked if anyone had the guts to bet for Gregson to lose. No one spoke.

Off to Calais for the France and Flanders Championship race

When I arrived for training, I felt all right and I managed some runs round the field with the top runners from Valenciennes and some others. We were told to be in good form to represent the Douai area at Calais on the 8th August 1919. So, I had a week to play with. I did long walks. My running was short, quick stuff of 440 yards or 880 yards. My longest run was three laps. I was training for speed. I knew I could stick the mile but it was speed I was short of.

I got down to Calais about 4.30pm on the Thursday and, in the mess, I met a Sergeant Colhone. He was an Army Champion shot putter. He was six feet two inches and fourteen stone and he was a fine athlete. He had me out after tea in Calais to a camp of the Irish Horse Depot. We met his pal, a Corporal cook, and we chatted. Then he brought three bowls of rice pudding, bread and butter and cheese and tea. Paddy Colhone said, 'Get on with it, Joe Binks.' He called me Joe, he was so happy go lucky.

Next day, I just ran 100 to 200 yards to try my spikes and to get the feel of the grass. I had a sharp walk with Paddy. He was full of fun, I liked him and one felt at home with him. On the day of the race, he said, 'Put all in this afternoon, Joe, don't leave it too late, go out to do it – win the 3pm game.'

He had already won the shot championship when he helped me with my gear. He examined the spikes and had the good idea to polish the soles and not leave anything to chance. My number eight was pinned on my back and front.

The South African Corporal was No. 11 stripped like before and wearing just shorts. There were only twelve runners in the race. Four areas each supplied their top three runners, twelve of the best in France and Flanders. As said, I was representing Douai. After we had answered our names and got our instructions, we got on the mark to start.

The Quartermaster shouted, 'Sir, a telegram for a Sergeant Gregson, King's Liverpool.' The starter was the red cap Officer, Major Brown, who was with us at Brussels. He said, 'Do you want it now or after the race, Gregson?'

I asked the Quartermaster to read it. He said, 'Wishing you the best of luck, your platoon Lieutenant.'

Right, at last someone remembered I was running for the King's Liverpool. It was a pleasant thought, all the same. You needed something to break the nerve-racking time waiting for your race.

Bang! We had four laps to do. I was off at the shot; clear in front at the first bend but it wasn't for long. The blonde chap got in front and away. I went with him as I thought what he could do, I could equal. I did it in the previous race, so we ran like that until the bell.

A tall athlete tried to come past but I ran faster and kept him behind. I was only two yards behind the Corporal, half-way through the last lap and I tried to get up into the lead but the Corporal wouldn't let me. He sprinted on. I couldn't sprint all out for 220 yards so I ran as fast as I could without sprinting. I lasted better and the Corporal started swaying so I sprinted for all I was worth. As Paddy had said, 'Don't leave it too late.'

With 20 yards to go, I passed him and, by five yards, I was the winner of the Mile at the France and Flanders Championship at Calais August 8th 1919. Swank? Yes, but true all the same.

Sergeant Paddy just picked me up like a cork and hugged 'his treat' as he said. Such a big man with a big smile.

The General presented me with a large silver medal. It had a battleground on one side and a target for firing on the other and a square left for it to be inscribed, which they did a few days later. This medal is also now in the Archives at the Lancashire Fusiliers museum in Bury.

That was it. There were no more bets and it was the final race as I thought.

A funny incident happened. Paddy put me down just near to that Quartermaster's table where we all had to wait for our medals.

A Lieutenant Price smacked me on the shoulder, 'Sergeant Gregson!' In turn, I said, 'Hello, Sir.' He said with his loud voice, 'Have you been running?'

'Yes, Sir.'

'I didn't see you, Sergeant.'

The Quartermaster heard this and knowing me, because of that telegram which he handed to me, then said to the Lieutenant, 'You did not see him?'

'No.' Lieutenant Price said.

'Why you must have seen him. Sergeant Gregson won and you were third only fifteen yards away!'

'Well, well and I didn't recognise you.'

We thought it funny. He said after, he was too worried during the race to give it much thought.

Actually, I had been too anxious wondering what that telegram was all about to worry about who I had to run against.

I got back to Douai and I was greeted a bit better this time.

Company Sergeant Major Bird met the train at the station with Bert, Jacko, Wilson, Sergeant Ashcroft and Sergeant Graham and A Company's Company Sergeant Major who was one of Big Jim's 'yes Sir, no Sir' men. He had been in hospital, sick. We stopped at an estaminet and celebrated for an hour. I reported in at the Battalions orderly room to be told, 'You are to report at the HQ officers' mess the first thing.' So, I washed and polished and went there.

The doctor let me in. He had expected me as they had enquired by telegram to the Sports Ground and knew it had finished by 4pm. It was now 8.30pm so they all knew the result. The Commanding Officer shook my hands saying, 'Don't think I have not been interested in your running success. Our doctor and Captain Nickels saw to that. We are all proud you have honoured our 4th Battalion King's Liverpool. We boast a champion and all share it.' They examined the medal. 'It is a medal to be proud of Sergeant Gregson.'

I went to B Company with Captain Nickels who was at HQ waiting for me to report, so when I got in B Company mess, our four Lieutenant platoon officers congratulated me. I told them we were on the mark when I was called out with a telegram from the Lieutenant.

'It bucked me up, Sir. I was on my own. I had no following like the others.'

Captain Nickels said, 'We all appreciate it, Sergeant. B Company will be told on parade.'

I told Captain Nickels that, in the morning, I had to report back to the training quarters at Calais, at 3.30pm at the latest on Monday if I get permission, Sir.'

'That I will see to at once,' said the Captain.

On 9th August 1919, *Major G.S. Brown, the Supt. Physical Training for British Troops in France & Flanders based at PT HQ at Wimereux, sent an order through to the 'Officer Commanding' 4th Battalion King's Liverpool Regiment.*

The order said, 'I beg to notify that the NCO mentioned below has been selected to represent Troops in France & Flanders at the Army Athletic Championship Meeting at Aldershot on August 28th & 29th and to request that he may be permitted to remain in Calais for training purposes until the team crosses to the United Kingdom on August 25th.

The NCO was me. My platoon Lieutenant asked me why I had to go back to Calais. 'All winners and second and third placed will represent France and Flanders at Aldershot on August 28th at the Army Finals for all our troops, no matter where they were stationed – Germany, France, Flanders, South Africa, Italy, India, Australia, New Zealand and in Great Britain. The runners would be the Champions from everywhere.'

I returned to Calais and Sergeant Colhone was waiting for me after tea. He took me out for a long walk calling round for our supper to that Corporal cook with his rice pudding and, do you know, I ate thin bread with butter with the pudding and I loved it.

We trained mostly on PT with a 'Jock' Sergeant drilling us all together. We didn't do anything like the amount of running I wanted, so I trained on. My idea, which I told Jock, was for the PT to keep me fit, and walking and running was to get me ready to race. I ran and walked all sorts, long and short, saunter and sweat.

We took the boat over to Aldershot and I went straight to bed. It was a rough crossing and I was terribly sick. I almost ruptured myself with nothing coming up but still wanting to be sick. I am sorry to write that, but it is what happened.

Sergeant Colhone looked after me with brandy. I didn't feel like breakfast. The worst thing was that my race was at 11am and I was not too good.

I came fourth only 20 yards behind the winner, Sergeant Thomas, a Welsh Guardsman with Corporal Schwartz second and an Indian chap third, only one yard in front of me.

Well, I hadn't done too badly from Barrow 1914 till Aldershot 1919. We all got fourteen days home leave. I reported back in the 1st week of September.

The end of running and near the end of my service

When I did get back to France about a hundred men all told had been demobbed. Our old 10th Lancashire Fusiliers were gone although Bert was still at Douai.

It looked as if not being married had something to do with some of the King's rules! Sergeant Jackson was due but not mentioned to go.

By October, I was put in charge of the Sergeants' mess. There was no more running now. All the Regiments were being sent home or, some like ours, being demobbed. I had one or two arguments with our Regimental Sergeant Major Big Jim which I won't mention.

On 10th November 1919, the daily orders were received. The last order being, 'Sergeant Gregson to be Temporary Company Sergeant-Major.'

Big Jim was a kind of meekness for a time. There were only 60 non-commissioned officers and men left. The officers too had gone including the doctor, Captain Nickels and Lieutenant Delmer.

We wondered what they would do with Bert and me as our time was not up till 25th February 1920 and it was the end of November 1919.

Then, suddenly we got orders to be out by 9am next morning to be demobbed. I said to Company Sergeant Major Bird that I couldn't be demobbed, 'My time is not until February.' It was then 22nd December.

'You are for Prees Heath,' he said and showed me his official list.

We got ordered to Cambrai Road Siding, Boulogne. Drummy waited to make sure no one was left. He knew we were on the move. If anyone was to stay behind, Drummy would not have gone with us. He was a knowing dog who didn't make a fuss. We stayed in the camp up the hill at Boulogne until the end of January 1920, just sleeping and eating with no parades and wondering what and where was next for us. We watched as hundreds and thousands were going on.

Bird had been asked by HQ to stay on and got to work straight away as a kind of orderly Sergeant. He was now dealing with complaints, meals, the daily routine and the sick and other matters.

The rest of us had nothing to do and would go into town until 10pm each day. One morning, Bird asked Bert if he wanted an office job with General HQ in Boulogne. Bert flew at it straight away. Dicky Bird told him to get to HQ for 10am tomorrow and added, 'Just go in casuals Bert and do let on that you know someone is wanted in the office. Tell them you are fed up at the camp as all NCOs are doing nothing.' After breakfast, Bert came back. He got the job thanks to Company Sergeant Major Bird who had told Bert about it even before he had posted the notice. Bert had experience, having done a similar job for the 10th Battalion Lancashire Fusiliers.

Bert had been adopted by a Blackpool couple who were the Mayor and Mayoress during the war. They had a mineral water business and, later in 1920, I visited them at their home just behind the Tower Buildings in Blackpool. They were originally from the Isle of Man.

Bert had told me that he wouldn't go back home to Blackpool to live. So, like me then, not having any ties, we could please ourselves. We could even sign on again!

Sergeants Ashcroft, Graham, Jackson and I used to meet Bert in a special estaminet. One evening, he was with a French lady about his age and he introduced her as Madame. She worked in the same job as Sergeant Bert, only with the French HQ, so it was natural for them to know each other.

Bert told me he liked her very much and she liked him. She had lost her husband, who had died of wounds in the war, so that was all right. You might as well enjoy life as best you can. We could see they were matched and both respected each other. Bert could speak French well and was good with his pen and was well educated. The last I heard, they did marry.

Now, the day came eventually when everyone was out on parade at 10am in full kit, set for England. But not Dicky Bird. He was indispensable demobbing everybody, even me, whose time didn't expire until February 25th.

Now, we had to leave Drummy. We asked him to stay but his ears were up and his tail was wagging away. Sergeant Graham had been feeding him and looking after him but even he failed. Drummy was saying, 'No! I'm coming with you.'

We marched down the hilly road from that camp. However, before we got to the boat's side, Drummy was back leading about eighty of us from all the ranks including Regimental Sergeant Major Big Jim, the Regimental Quartermaster and Company Sergeant Major, Sergeants, Non-commissioned officers and Privates. We put our packs down by the railway coaches nearest to our gangway. Drummy had got under one of the coaches, hiding.

Two military policemen red caps came up to us, 'Where did your dog go?' Sergeant Ashcroft replied, 'What are you complaining about?'

'You brought a dog with you.'

'Half a dozen dogs more like,' he said 'and they brought us! Which one do you want?'

'Yours,' one of the red caps said.

'My pack is here; look in it if you think I have got a dog.'

'Funny aren't you, Sergeant'

'No, I think it's you trying to be funny.'

We got orders to pick up our packs and get on board by command of the ship's captain through a microphone. We got on slowly; all wondering what would happen to that dog. We daren't look back that way towards the dog and, on board, we stayed on the top deck, squinting on shore but we couldn't see Drummy. He had gone.

The two red caps came on board and spoke to the ship's officer. One of them started a search of the ship, starting at our end. We had put our equipment on a large coil of big rope which was hollow in the centre. We sat on top of the coils and after about ten minutes or so, Drummy came up the stairway slyly. He then ran, jumped up the ropes and down into the centre of the coil and out of sight. We all thought the dog must have come onto the ship lower down with about 80 women, WAAF, Wrens and nurses with their skirts hiding him.

The boat started out half an hour late. At Dover, we whispered down to Drummy, 'Well, old lad, we are off again.' He looked up at us as we put on our things, he knew we were going. We got off the ship last and walked up the station platform as our railway coach was last, with the guard's van on the very end. We put our things in our compartment.

The ship's officer came along and spoke to the guard who then shouted for two porters. So, another search started with the guard taking our last coach. In each compartment, he used his flag stick to sweep under the seats. He got to ours, searched and then said, 'It would save time if you told us where your dog is.' 'At Boulogne,' Sergeant Ashcroft replied, 'with all the others that marched down to the boat.'

We had all given up hope for Drummy, when he leapt up between the two last coaches of the train, onto the platform, jumped into our coach, almost knocking Sergeant Graham down, stood in the doorway and then darted under the seat. That's the sort of dog he was, not a bark, not a sign, hidden, even weighing up the form, he was on his own.

Luck was with us and Drummy and our coaches arrived at Prees Heath.

At our camp, everyone got out and the doors were left open. We filed, about two hundred all told, into a big hut and passed through giving up our equipment and our particulars. Drummy was with the other 'strays' in that camp. He was being fed by the cooks at the cook house and we waited until he had finished. We got him a drink and into our hut for the night.

The next morning, we were given suits or we could take the money instead. I took the money. Drummy was clinging to Sergeant Graham and me as we were the only two in uniform. Four of us got on the train bound for Liverpool via Warrington. Two men got out at Crewe, leaving in our compartment just the two of us and an old lady who got on at Crewe. Bank Quay, Warrington, was just a few minutes away.

I was up ready to get out and asked that dog to come home with me, to a good home. With his ears pricked up and his tail wagging, he again said, 'No!' The lady tried to encourage him but that was it.

Drummy was bound for Liverpool and I was bound for home.

Army Form W. 5112.

RECORD OFFICE, Preston

17. 5. 1921.

I am directed to transmit the accompanying Oak Leaf Emblem which has been awarded to you in respect of your services with the

KING'S REGT. LIVERPOOL

I am to request that you will be so good as to acknowledge the receipt of the decoration on the attached form, which is to be returned to the above address in the enclosed addressed envelope, which needs no stamp.

I am,
Your obedient Servant,

For Officer i/c
Infantry Record Office, PRESTON.
i/c Records.

In May 1921, Grandpa was awarded the Oak Leaf Emblem for his Mention in Despatches

Grandpa, back home, where he went to work as a maltster for Greenall Whitley brewery in Warrington even though he was tee-total himself

Grandpa loved all sports especially Rugby League and Cricket where he played locally

Grandpa, the father

Grandpa, the man

Grandpa with Grandma. She was not part of the war story but very much part of his life – his love, his comfort and his confidante

Grandpa with his children and grandchildren including me at the front failing to have done up all my buttons and Grandma holding onto my arm

Grandpa as I remember him. Wrapped up warm to watch his grandchild play rugby at school

ADDENDA

Obituary (from Local Warrington newspaper)

Friday September 28th 1979
Mr G. A. Gregson

The funeral took place on Tuesday last week of Mr George Alfred Gregson, husband of Mrs Dorothy Gregson, 365 Wilderspool Causeway, Warrington. He died at the age of 89 on September 12th at the home of his daughter in St. Annes-on-Sea. A service at Our Lady's Church preceded internment at Warrington Cemetery. Rev Father J Daley of Our Lady's and the Rev Father Sharrock of the Church of Our Lady, Star of the Sea, St. Annes, officiated.

Mr. Gregson was born in Widnes but lived in Warrington for 65 years and was a maltster with Greenall Whitley & Co for 40 years. He was in the Lancashire Fusiliers, rising to Sergeant Major in the First World War, serving on the Somme, at Ypres, the Dardenelles and Gallipoli, where he was mentioned in despatches. He was a member of the Auxiliary Fire Service during the Second World War. He joined the staff of Greenall Whitley immediately after the First World War.

A well-known local sportsman, he was a member of Warrington Harriers and Runcorn and District Harriers. He was a distance runner of note becoming Northern Cross-Country champion, runner-up in the All England Championship and also ran for England in France while in the Army. He was known in local cricket and rugby circles and coached the Greenall Whitley rugby team.

He leaves a son, two daughters, twelve grandchildren and four great grandchildren.

The funeral was attended by many relatives, friends, and parishioners of Our Lady's and former colleagues of Greenall Whitley & Co Ltd.

Weekly News – Local Paper Report – 1915

Widnes Soldier-Athlete's Success
Lance-Corporal Gregson Wins Cross-Country Race at Barrow

Widnes was well-presented in a recent regimental harrier's race at Barrow-in-Furness, where a large number of troops of various regiments are quartered. Lance-Corporal A Gregson, of the 4th Lancashire Fusiliers, and of Bank Street, Widnes, carried off the individual championship, and the team of eight which he captained won second place.

Twelve teams competed over a course of six miles, a start being made from Cavendish Park, the Barrow N.U. Football Ground.

Gregson took the lead after about two miles had been covered, beating a Borderer who had so far had the advantage.

Gregson's time was 31 minutes 15 seconds – 92 seconds before the second man. Gregson won a medal and £2 and a watch to the value of £3 5 shillings. The team prize for second being 5 shillings each.

Gregson had a great reception from the men in his company. 'I shall never forget the way the boys treated me,' he writes to his sister. 'The Officers are treating our men to free seats at the Palace (bow-wow!). We only had a fortnight to get ready for it. Some of the other teams were in the know before us. Thanks to my knowledge of team running, all our men finished well.'

Appended is a list of Gregson's former successes: Liverpool & District Championship at Bebington (7 miles), Ex-West Lancashire Junior Championship at Lancaster (7 miles), third twice in the Warrington Harriers' Christmas Handicap, the Senior Point Championship, Police & Tradesmen's Mile, off 130 yards.

Weekly News – Local Paper Report August 17th, 1917

Another Success By a Widnes Athlete
During last winter, Sergeant A Gregson, Lancashire Fusiliers, won the cross-country championship of his regiment. He has also shown his quality at a short distance by winning the mile championship of his Battalion, also running the 880 yards in the relay race, which his company team won.

A week later the Brigade held their sports. Sergeant Gregson entered the open mile and he again proved a success by winning. He was also picked in the Battalion relay team, which the Lancashire Fusiliers, won, Gregson again running the 880 yards distance.

Two days after this, the division signallers held their sports, with three open events – the mile, quarter-mile and obstacle race. Sergeant Gregson was sent to represent his regiment for the mile with Private

Dyson to run the quarter-mile and Private Bowers, the obstacle race. Out of the three events, the Lancashire Fusiliers won two firsts and a third.

Gregson ran a splendid race, and won by 70 yards, Holmes (Surrey A.C.) being second. Dyson ran a good race and won the quarter by 3 yards. Bowers ran third in the obstacle race.

In another inter-Battalion sports, Gregson hopes to notch another win for his Battalion and 'good old Widnes.'

There are also four other Gregson brothers serving their country: Sergeant Jim, Canadian Forces, France, Albert Edward, Minesweepers, Ralph, Bdr, Salonika Force (Lancashire Fusiliers), Robert, HMS *Dreadnought*.

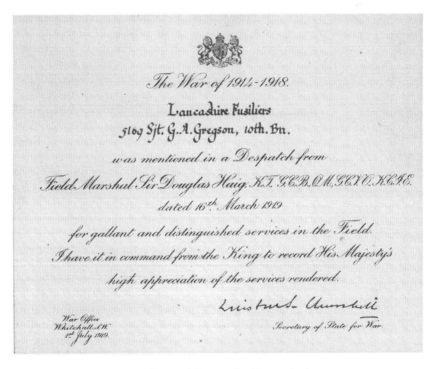

Grandpa was 'Mentioned in Despatches'
for gallant and distinguished services in the Field

10th Battalion War Diary entries for the first month of the Battle of the Somme, the Battle of Arras and the Last Days of the War

KEY (where known):
Bn = Battalion
Coy = Company
LG = Lewis Gun
MG = Machine Gun
O.R's = Other Ranks
WR = West Riding
WRR = West Riding Regiment
NF = Northumberland Fusiliers
LF = Lancashire Fusiliers
D of W's = Duke of Westminsters
(U/K) = UNKNOWN word in the diary, that is, the editor was unable to read the word written

The first month of the Battle of the Somme
Written by: Major G.L. Torrens

July 1916

Place	Date	Time	Details
Morlancourt	2nd		March to Morlancourt
	3rd		Move up into action
	4th–5th		On the night of the 4th/5th July, Shelter Alley and Quadrangle Trench were carried by two companies 10th LF's, one company remaining in support at the hedge connecting Shelter and Bottom Woods and one in reserve at Crucifix Trench. The attacking companies were received with rifle and MG fire but rushed the trenches. Capt Thacker personally reconnoitred Quadrangle trench almost as far as Contalmaison and established a stop in the trench. This stop was afterwards driven in. The position remained essentially unaltered during 5th and 6th.

Place	Date	Time	Details
	6th	4pm	During the afternoon of the 6th Lieutenant Clay reconnoitred Pearl Alley and after a successful fight with some German bombers, he established stops at the junction of Pearl Alley and Quadrangle trench. There stops were driven in by the Germans about 10pm.
	7th	2am	At 2am, the Battalion advanced on Quadrangle Support trench having one company in reserve at Shelter Alley. During the advance, the German stops in Pearl Alley were cut off and prisoners captured. On nearing Quadrangle support trench the Battalion was received with heavy rifle and MG fire and driven back. The right company in contact with the Northumberland Fusiliers fell back to Quadrangle trench. The two left companies however managed to establish themselves in Pearl Alley and held on until daybreak. Two small parties in all 30 men found themselves in Contalmaison and claim to have destroyed 4 MG's by firing into the works. They captured 20 prisoners and returned to their companies in Pearl Alley at daylight bringing a MG back. At about 4am, a detachment of the Worcester Regiment arrived in Pearl Alley to make an attack on Contalmaison but, at this moment, the enemy counter-attacked from Quadrangle Support and from Contalmaison and both regiments were driven back into Quadrangle trench.
		8am	The situation remained unchanged during and after the attack by the WR Regiment and the Manchester Regiment.
		10am	Lieutenant Col Wade, 10th LF's, went to Quadrangle trench and found the trench containing WR Regt, Manchesters and 10th LF's considerably mixed. The NF were more to the right. At this time, the enemy were making bombing attacks from Contalmaison and bombers of all corps were sent to (U/K) them which were successfully done.

Place	Date	Time	Details
		Noon	About midday, an attack was made on Contalmaison by the Welsh Regiment and Lieutenant Pratt of that Regt sending back to say there were two companies of that regiment holding on to the edge of the village but unable to advance for want of support, the reserve company from the LF's from Shelter trench and a large number of Welsh and Worcesters from the same trench were sent (U/K). The village I understand was carried.
		5pm	The Battalion was relieved by the South Staffords and Sherwood Foresters moving to Meaulte
Villers sous Ailly	16th		Battalion training and re-organisation
Hangest	23rd		Entrain and march to Buire sur Ancre
Buire sur Ancre	24th–31st		Battalion in bivouac. Bayonet fighting. Physical Training, Route Marching and Training generally. In Corps reserve.

The Battle of Arras 9th April to 17th May 1917
Written By Major G.L. Torrens

April 1917

Place	Date	Time	Details
Sus-St Leger	1st–5th		Schemes. Cavalry in touch with enemy rearguard. Battalion acting Advance Guard to Brigade
	5th		Move by march route to Denier
Denier	8th		Move by march route to Wanquetin
Wanquetin	9th		Move by route march to Arras. On arrival the Battalion occupied cellars and old homes at the extreme eastern end of the town within a few hundred yards of where our front line had been that morning. It snowed during the journey and was generally unpleasant.
Arras	10th		Battalion in cellars etc

Place	Date	Time	Details
	11th		On the evening of this day, the Battalion moved out in a heavy snowfall to occupy reserve line trenches. After a journey of three miles in as many hours the Battalion bivouacked in a field for four hours and were afterwards led into the Brown line, the northern point of which was at Feuchy. Here the Battalion occupied German trenches in comparative quietness.
	12th		With the forward movement of artillery and transport a portion of which settled down close to the trenches of the Battalion, came a certain liveliness on the part of the enemy which developed during the day.
	13th		The enemy had now brought up a large number of guns to replace those he had lost on the 9th and to strengthen his position and with these he poured out an unceasing volume of shellfire doing a certain amount of damage to the trenches on our right. Aerial activity was a marked feature and several exciting combats took place each side sending a number of the other to the ground. In the evening, the enemy commenced shelling the Brown line and the area immediately west of it with gas shells. These he sent at a steady rate throughout the night the number being estimated at about 7,000. The shells had only an immediate local effect and the number of casualties in the Battalion was comparatively slight – 2 Killed 9 gassed wounded and 3 wounded.
	14th		Brown Line. The enemy's shelling was moderate and no unusual incident occurred. Battalion moved into Support line trenches north side of Orange Hill.
	15th		No unusual incident
	16th		B & D Coys cut a communication trench from the railway to the front line. A German pigeon carrying a message arrived at Brigade Headquarters. Lieutenant-Col Wade DSO deciphered the message as follows: Despatched By K.T.K C. North Received by pigeon post carriage date 16.4.17 time 4.36pm pigeon number 16 and 54 'The fire upon (U/K) line has somewhat decreased. The (U/K) fire falls upon the (U/K) southwest of Riencourt (presumed 24 U/K) Strong English reconnaissance K.T.K C. North

Place	Date	Time	Details
	17th		The enemy shelling was comparatively slight on our trenches during the day. In the evening, the Battalion relieved the 9th West Riding Regt in the front line. A Coy continued work on the trench commenced by B and D Coys.
	18th		The Battalion was relieved by the 8th South Staffs and marched to the caves at Arras arriving early on the morning of the 19th
	19th		Caves St. Sauvier, Arras
	20th		The Battalion moved into the Brown Line on the afternoon of this day taking up the centre position which had been occupied by the 7th Border Regt.
	21st		The Battalion relieved the 9th Northern Ireland Fusiliers in the Southern portion of the Brown Line.
	22nd		The Battalion provided carrying parties to the Northumberland Fusiliers and to the T.M.B
	23rd		On the evening of this day, Capt Pegram and 3 other Officers went with about 140 men carried food water and supplies to the Northumberland Fusiliers in the front line. The shelling was very heavy and the party was frequently broken and recollected. All stores were delivered but the party was unable to get back before daybreak and did not rejoin the Battalion till the evening of the 24th.
	24th		At 12.15am, the Battalion was ordered to move to Monchy to take over a portion of the front held by the 29th Division. After a strenuous time during which 2Lt Mercer was wounded and several men killed and wounded by heavy shell fire, the Battalion reached Monchy but had to return to the Brown Line as it was now considered, owing to approaching daylight, to be expedient to relieve.
	25th		The Battalion was relieved by the 9th Royal Fusiliers at midnight. 2 Coys under Major ffComyn dug a communication trench to Rifle trench and rejoined the Battalion at Arras at about 6am on the 26th
Arras	26th		Arras moved by motor bus to Sus-St-Leger
Sus-St-Leger	30th		Battalion training
			Reinforcements in April: Officers 2 O/R's 131
			Casualties in April: Officers 2 O/R's 80

May 1917

Place	Date	Time	Details
	1st		Bus to Hautes-Avesnes
Hautes-Avesnes	2nd		March to G.17 a (St. Nicholas). The Battalion remained in Brigade Reserve and was employed in working and carrying parties till the 9th when it moved up in to Brigade Support
	9th–11th		In support in a railway cutting
	11th		Battalion relieved 9th (S) Bn W.R.R in trenches South-east of Gavrelle and the following morning attacked at 6.30am Charlie trench. A Coy under Capt Barrow and part of B Coy under Major Comyn succeeded in affecting an entrance but were driven out by strong hostile bombing parties. The Battalion suffered following casualties: 13 Officers – 226 O/R's.
Cutting	17th–19th		After 6 days in Brigade Support the Battalion returned to the railway cutting remaining there two days and again moving up on the 19th in relief of the 7th Lincoln Regt. This tour lasted 3 days in spite of (U/K) shelling on the part of the enemy we only suffered three casualties.
	22nd		Relieved by 6th Dorset Regt in return to cutting
	27th		Relieve 9th W.R. Regt in Brigade Support in the Green Line at Fampoux. Gavrelle Line. Hurrum and Helford trenches
	29th		Relieved By 25th S Bn NF 34th Division, returned to camp at St. Nicholas and entrained that day for Saulty
	30th		Thence marched to Humbercourt
Humbercourt	31st		Resting
			Total Casualties for May: 15 Officers 241 O/R's
			Total Reinforcements: 10 Officers 43 O/R's

The Last Days of the War

Written By Major T. B. Forwood (October) and Lieutenant-Col G. L. Torrens (November)

October 1918

Place	Date	Time	Details
Rocquigny	1st		Battalion in rest & training
	5th		Moved from Rocquigny to Equancourt
Equancourt	8th	05:00	Moved from Equancourt to sunken road S of Gouzecourt (Q.B.c)
Gouzecourt		17:30	Moved to trenches E of Gonnolieo
	9th	01:50	Moved to Montecouvez Farm
		09:30	Moved to Angle Chateau
		18:15	Moved to Sorval Chateau. Passed through Selvigny which was occupied by civilians
Sorval Chateau	10th	03:30	Received orders that Division would attack on a Brigade frontage two Bn's in line pushing forward in seven bounds, the final objective being high ground K10, K3 & E26, N.E of Neuilly. 50th Brigade would attack with 51st in support. 52nd in Reserve. The Division would be in position By 05:20 hours
		4:30	Moved from Sorval Chateau O.20.ac to take position in support to the Manchester. 1,000 (U/K) in rear.
		05:10	Arrived in position O15c.9.8. (Cross roads of Caullery)
		07:30	Followed up the attack moving in Coys in Artillery Formation. A Coy on right. B Coy on left supported by C Coy and D Coy respectively. The Bn moved in N.E direction and arrived at Montigny O.12 at 08:30am. News was received that the 'Manchesters' were pushing on, so after ten minutes halt, progress was continued still moving N.E. arriving at La Sucrerie, S.E. of Inchy at 11.30am. During the last 1,000 yards …
Inchy		11.30am	the formation of the Bn was altered to Platoon in Artillery formation. The distance covered was approximately 6 1/3 miles.

Place	Date	Time	Details
		13:00	Referral received that Manchester Regt were consolidating along the River Ircluin J.22 & J23. The enemy about this time began shelling the village of Troisville with Blue Gas shells. Received instructions to take up a position in J27 & J32 as a protection to the right flank.
		13:45	Taken up new position Bn HQ J27.B.3.2 (Cross Roads South of Beaumont & S.E. of Audencourt)
		17:00	At 17:00, an attack was made on Neuilly by the W. Yorks Regt. The attack was carried out under a (U/K) barrage of light field guns and machine guns but was not altogether successful
		18:30	During the afternoon and evening, the enemy shelled the villages of Troisville, Beaumont & Inchy and at noon enemy planes were active. Several large fires were observed N of Inchy, probably in neighbourhood of Quievy & St. Hilaire-Les-Cambrai.
	11th		Bn was standing by to relieve if necessary Battalion of 51st Brigade
	12th	01:15	Bn left to take up a position S of Neuvilly preparatory to an attack at 05:00.

Place	Date	Time	Details
Neuvilly		04:00	Bn in support. A Coy had orders to follow close behind the D of W's Regt which was attacking on the South side of the village and when the leading Bn was over the river A Coy was ordered to clear the village N of the river working from S.E. to N.W. Similarly, B Coy following the Manchester Regt were to clear the village from N.W. to S.E. Both Coys on completion were to occupy a position N of the Railway behind the Manchester Regt & act as support in event of counter-attack. The 2 remaining Coys C in the right and D Coy on the left to occupy positions on K7 & K14 & could be called upon by A & B Coys respectively if requiring assistance to clear the village. B, C and D Coys were in position by 04:00 hours the two latter digging in. A Coy following the D of W's were late but eventually got to their position just before 05:00 hours. Enemy (U/K) shelling the valley with gas & C Coy was ordered before zero hour to move up in close support of A Coy. Zero hour for attacking & clearing the village was 06:00. MG & Artillery being kept on the village until that hour.
		05:00	Artillery barrage opened A & B Coys followed the D of W's Regt & the Manchester Regt respectively. C Coy following A Coy. The D of W's did not get their rear platoons over the river before enemy barrage came down. A & C Coys did not get across.
Neuvilly		05:50	The enemy were still holding positions on the South side of the river with MG's & sniper posts although this side was supposed to be clear.
		05:48	C Coy began clearing out these nests & killed several of the enemy. The house to house fighting was difficult but those of the enemy that were not killed escaped over the bridge at K8.a.7.7. O.C. A Coy was wounded & 2Lt W. Davidson M.C was sent from Bn HQ to command the Coy.

Place	Date	Time	Details
		08:00	The D of W's advance troops were in the line of the road South of the railway in K.9.a.c. but the rear troops were still S of the river. Consequently, A & C Coys were unable to cross. MG fire was intense from the railway and Southern edge of the village which was particularly focussed on the bridges by which the forward Bn had crossed. A & C Coys dug in on roads K8.c & K8.d.2.3 and prepared to get across when they could. B Coy got over the river behind the Manchester Regt and at 06:00 hours started to clear the village from N.W. There was considerable opposition from S.E. of the cemetery. This Coy took 30 odd prisoners by the time it reached a N & S through the Church & had killed many of the enemy
		08:30	The situation was as follows: D Coy was attached to the Manchester Regt which was for its final objective on the ridge N of the railway & was ordered to take up a position in Quarry K1.d & two platoons on high ground K1.d.0.5 One of these platoons mopped up the cemetery into which some of the enemy had returned from the railway.
Neuvilly		08:30	B Coy had mopped up 2/3rds of the village. A & C Coys held up K8.c & K8.a after trying to get into village by bridge opposite church. Heavy MG fire on K9.a-d from railway & southern outskirts of the village. 33 wounded had by this time passed through R.A.P. which was situated at Bn HQ K13.B.15.45
		09:00	B Coy had cleared most of the village but was held up by MG fire from the tunnel K9.a. They by then moved to its allotted position in K2 central. There had been very stiff fighting in the village and nearly 50 prisoners had been taken. Later D Coy received orders from O.C. Manchester Regt to cross the railway & work N.E. direction to clear the factory. This Coy at the time had made good the line of the railway with two platoons behind the Manchester Regt
		12:00	3 Officers – 45 O.R. had passed through R.A.P.

Place	Date	Time	Details
		12:50	A & C Coy were sent orders to mop up the village entering from N to S working in conjunction with B Coy. B Coy met a large party of the enemy at the entrance to the village which it scattered with LG fire. The enemy had dribbled back into the village from the railway & through the tunnel previously mentioned.
		15:00	The enemy delivered a strong counter-attack on the Manchester Regt & drove them off the ridge. The attack was proceeded by a heavy artillery barrage. The Coys were in the following positions: B Coy beginning to pass through the village. A & C Coy over the river on the N of the village & ready to follow B Coy. D Coy 2 platoons advancing on the factory & 2 near the quarry. The counter-attack was stopped and many casualties caused in the enemy's ranks from artillery fire & MG. 4 of the latter came into action at Bn HQ & 4 more in K13.B on the ridge driving out the attacking troops. The enemy succeeded in regaining the village & railway but were prevented from crossing the river by the 4 Coys A, B, C and D in the quarry & bank K1 a-d. Some of the Manchester Regt from the ridge were also there & the remainder in support behind with defensive flanks K1.d.e. Coys reorganised
		17:00	Orders received from the Manchester Regt to hold the bank & quarry N of the river & Lancs Fusiliers to hold all the line of the river on the South denying all crossing of the river to the enemy. C & A Coys were sent to clear the village South of the river again in order to be certain that none of the enemy had got across & were concealed in the houses. None of the enemy was encountered but strong MG fire was met from the Northern bank. Posts were established at suitable points guarding the river as far as K8B.6.0 where an international post was formed with the D of W's Regt

Place	Date	Time	Details
Neuvilly		24:00	During the night, the line was taken over by the Sherwood Foresters & 7th Lincolns 51st Brigade but none of the actual posts were relieved. The 51st Briagde being in position, the Bn was ordered to withdraw to billets at Inchy, the last Coy getting back about 06:45 13th inst
			Casualties: KILLED 33 O.R.s WOUNDED 4 Officers 134 O.R.s MISSING 15 O.R.s. The Bn went into line with 20 Officers & 558 O.R.s and came out with 16 Officers & 364 O.R.s Prisoners claimed: 2 Officers 47 O.R.s Communication by (U/K) was kept up with all 4 Coys throughout the day & no lines were laid. Communication with Brigade presented no difficulty on the Brigade R.C. Bn HQ were in the same dug-out. Casualties were particularly amongst the Coy signallers & stretcher bearers. Wounded were quickly evacuated. Visibility all day was exceedingly bad but the Artillery liaison was excellent. A light T.M. attached to A & B Coys did excellent work. Several (U/K) were seen in the village.
Inchy	17th	16:00	Bn relieved the 6th Dorsets who were occupying a line in the Neuvilly in Platoon posts. D Coy were on the right on road K8.a.4.2 – K8.a.8.8. A Coy in centre and B Coy in left, North of river Selle K1.d.0.7. C Coy were in support & BHQ at S.11.d.35.20. Relief was completed by 21:50 hours. One artillery was active throughout the night.
Neuvilly	18th		Certain amount of activity on both sides
	19th		Quiet day. A little MG & Artillery activity

Place	Date	Time	Details
		20:15	B & C Coys relieved by 6th Dorsets. A & D Coys remained in position until 20th inst to prevent the enemy crossing to South side of river during the attack by the 50th Brigade on morning of 20th inst. B & C Coys & BHQ returned to Inchy at 21:00 hours
	20th	02:00	Attack on Neuvilly. Heavy artillery bombardment on Corps from 02:00 to 04:00 and incessant fire till 07:30 hours. Attack carried out by 50th Brigade, the 51st Brigade passing through.
		07:15	B & C Coys moved into the area J.11d & J.12c. A & D Coy remained in their position till 15:00 hours. Village was subjected to heavy gas shelling. A & D Coys were treated for gas on coming out of the line at 16:00 hours.
		18:00	Bn moved into rest at Inchy
Inchy	21st	05:00	Orders to 'stand to' at 05:00. Stood to but no further orders received. Bn under orders at half hours notice.
		09:00	Warning order that Brigade would relieve 51st Brigade in the line this evening.
		22:00	Relieved Notts & Derbys in area E.27.c BHQ K2.B.4. A large amount of gas shelling took place during the relief
Neuvilly	22nd		Artillery active throughout the day
	23rd	18:00	Relieved by 6th Leicesters (21st Division) and returned to Audencourt arriving by 22:00
Audencourt	24th		Resting
	25th	08:30	Moved from Audencourt to billets in Beaumont
Beaumont	26th	08:30	Moved from Beaumont to position E of Ovillers. E23.a. & E.23B (SW of road)
		18:00	Moved from Ollivers to Poix du Nord relieving the 1st (U/K) (21st Division) in the line. Arrived at BHQ X21.d.8.6 at 19:00 hours. Major Forwood in command, Relief completed by 21:10 hours. Front line was approximately road X11.a. X11.c & X14.B with outposts E of road. Enemy using gas shells freely
	27th		Wiring & consolidations of posts.
	28th		Much artillery & aeroplane activity
	29th	18:00	Bn relieved by 2nd Lincolns Regt (21st Division) returning to billets in Ollivers

Place	Date	Time	Details
	30th		In rest and training at Ollivers. Lieutenant-Col G. L. Torrens resumed command.
	31st		Ditto
			Casualties for the Month:
			Officers – Killed 1 Wounded 7
			O.Rs – Killed 44 Wounded 184 Missing 3
			Reinforcements for the month:
			Officers – 15
			O.R.s – 306

November 1918

Place	Date	Time	Details
Ovillers SW of Louvigines	1st		Bn rested during the day
	2nd		Bn relieved the 2n Bn the Leicesters Regt (21st Division) in the front line SW of Louvigines
	3rd		During the morning, verbal orders were received that the Bn would attack through the Foret de Mormal & capture the line, S.9.c.5.0.- S.15.a.8.0 At dusk, Bn HQ moved up to Petit Gay Farm and all preparations for the attack in the morning were completed, advanced posts being slightly withdrawn in order to escape our own barrage.
	4th	01:00	The Bn assembled on a general line X.17.B.60.95, X.17.d.95.60 in the following order: C & D Coy from right to left) in front with B & A Coy in close support. At 05:30 hours, the barrage opened & remained on enemy front line for 4 minutes when the Bn attacked, each coy being on a 2 platoon frontage with 2 in close support. Day broke about 05:45 with an extremely heavy ground mist. Little opposition was encountered up to the copse, X.18.a.5.8, which D Coy quickly rushed & captured the Garrison. C Coy on the right first encountered resistance in copse S.13.d. The 2 leading platoons succeeded in rushing the posts & pushed on towards Futoy.

Place	Date	Time	Details
	4th	01:00	At 06:06 hours, the Louvigines Road was reached, the left leading coy passing La Motte Farm a few minutes later, leaving its support coy to mop up. At this time heavy MG fire was encountered from the farm building. Lewis Guns were brought into action & one platoon detailed to rush the farm.
The remainder of the Coy moved to the east side of the buildings & were in time to capture several of the enemy emerging from an outhouse. No difficulties were experienced in helping close up to the barrage & the advance was now fairly rapid. Opposition from the western edge of Futoy was overcome by leading Coy and after the barrage had lifted from the line of the road – S.14.a & c. The advance continued.
Immediately, after the support Coy had crossed the road & mopped up the village, the enemy barrage (which had been previously falling in vicinity of jumping off positions) came down on the road.
Futoy was captured at 07:05 hours.
Hostile artillery activity was now increasing, and sides and tracks were severely searched. Coys reached the final objective at 08:00 hours & immediately consolidated east of this line.
Platoon posts were formed & the left support Coy established an International post at cross roads S.8.c.9.1. Whilst digging in Coys were subjected to shelling from the left & desultory MG fire from North of Pont A Vache. The protective barrage remained for 30 minutes to enable the 51st Brigade to form up & pass through, followed later by the 50th Brigade.
The 52nd Brigade was now in Divisional Reserve, the Bn moving into billets in Futoy in the evening.
Futoy	5th–6th		The Bn remained in Reserve, and except for a little salvage work rested all the time.
Berlaimont	7th		The Bn moved by march route to Berlaimont via Locquignol & La Tete Noir arriving at 14:00 hours

Aulnoye	8th	08:00	The Bn moved to Aulnoye, staying in billets until evening, when orders were issued for a further attack. Consequently, the Bn moved about 22:30 hours to Limonte Fontaine to relieve the 7th Lincolns. The objective being the village of Beaufort. The march up was exceedingly quiet, not a shell from the enemy being heard. On arrival at Limonte Fontaine, information was received that the enemy had withdrawn, & that one Coy of the 7th Lincolns, following up the enemy, had established itself in Beaufort. A Coy was now detailed as advance guard to the Bn & proceeded to Beaufort finding no sign of the enemy. The other 3 Coys now followed and an outpost line was established about 1 mile east of the village, with B Coy as outpost coy, A & D Coys forming a defensive flank on the left with C Coy in support.
	9th	08:00	Cavalry patrols were pushed through the outpost line, but were unable to make contact with the enemy.
		15:00	In the afternoon, A, C & D Coys were withdrawn to billets in the village. 'B' Coy remaining on the outpost line.
	10th	06:00	D Coy relieved B Coy in the outpost line, B Coy moving back into the village.
	11th	08:00	Wire received stating that the enemy had agreed to the conditions of the armistice as laid down by the Allies & that hostilities would cease at 11:00 hours today. About 12:30 hours, the Bn moved to Berliamont, this being the first stage of the journey back to Inchy.
Vendegies	12th	09:00	Bn marched to Vendegies Au Bois via Foret de Mormal & Enclefontaine
Inchy	13th	09:00	Bn completed the march to Inchy via Ollivers Ameral remaining there for the rest of the month. Whilst at Inchy, salvage work was energetically carried out, at least one Coy per day being always employed. Many kinds of sport were organised including football matches, paper chases etc.
	26th	14:30	The Bn as part of the 52nd Brigade group was inspected by the Divisional Commander Orders & also full marching orders
	30th	10:30	The Divisional Commander presented ribbons to all W.O.s, NCO's and men who had gained awards during the recent advance.

Following casualties were suffered during the month:

2Lt R.C. Lee – Killed

2Lt F.H. Irwell – Wounded

2Lt – W. Davidson MC – Wounded

2Lt R. M Nesbit _ Wounded – Gas

2Lt J.L. Martin (U/K) – Wounded Gas

Other ranks: 9 Killed, 178 Wounded 8 Missing

Estimated No of prisoners taken: 212

Receipts obtained for: 146

Heavy machine guns captured: 6

Light machine guns captured: 11

Trench mortar: 1

'The History of the Lancashire Fusiliers 1914–1918'

Calendar of Moves during George Alfred Gregson service

Records show that Grandpa, following his training with the 4th Battalion LF's at Barrow, disembarked on 18/07/1915 and joined the 1st Battalion LF's:

The official records show the following moves for the 1st Battalion LF's:

12th–21st July	Lemnos
22nd–27th July	Gully Beach
27th–4th Aug	Trenches, Hampshire Cut, Krithia
4th–6th Aug	Gully Beach
6th–14th Aug	Trenches, Eski Line
14th–19th Aug	Gully Beach
19th Aug	SS *Clacton* to Suvla Bay
20th–22nd Aug	Chocolate Hill, Suvla, attack Hill 112 on 21st August
22nd–31st Aug	Reserve, Salt Lake, Suvla
31st–8th Sept	Trenches, Kuchuk, Anafarta, Suvla
9th Sept	SS *Osmanieh* to Imbros
9th–21st Sept	Imbros
21st Sept	SS *Ermine* and *Redbreast* to Suvla Bay
21st–26th Sept	Reserve, Lancashire Terraces, Suvla Bay
26th–30th Sept	Support, Suvla Bay

30th–28th Nov	Trenches, Suvla Bay, disastrous blizzard and flood, 26th Nov
28th–2nd Dec	Reserve, Suvla Bay
2nd–13th Dec	Trenches, Suvla Bay
13th–14th Dec	Reserve, Suvla Bay
14th Dec	SS *Barry* to Mudros
15th Dec	Mudros
16th Dec	Transhipped to SS *Southland* and SS *Brighton* to Helles
16th–18th Dec	Krithia Road, Helles
18th–31st Dec	Rest Area, X Beach, Helles

Grandpa moved into an Australian hospital bell tent on or around 29th November 1915

Following a period back in England, Grandpa was sent back to France to join the 10th Battalion Lancashire Fusiliers. Grandpa only left convalescence in Dartford in April. He got 14 days leave, a quick visit to Hull and then back to Barrow.

Grandpa mentions arriving at Boulogne and then marching to a farm where he met the 10th Battalion at Boisdinghem. The official records for the 10th Battalion from 19th May 1916 onwards:

19th May–11th June	Boisdinghem
11th June	Entrained Audruicq
12th June	Detrained Longeau, Coisy.
13th June	Heilly
14th–23rd June	Boie des Tailles, Etinehem
23rd–28th June	Trenches, Mametz
28th–2nd July	Bois des Tailles
2nd–3rd July	Morlancourt
3rd–7th July	In action, Contalmaison (Shelter Alley, Quadrangle Trench, Pearl Alley)
7th July	Meaulte
8th July	Ville-sur-Ancre
10th–15th July	Riencourt
15th–23rd July	Villers-sous-Ailly

23rd July	By train, Hangest to Buire-sur-l'Ancre
24th–31st July	Reserve, Buire-sur-l'Ancre
1st–4th Aug	Reserve, Montauban Alley
4th–8th Aug	Support, Pommiers Trench, Montauban
8th–10th Aug	Fricourt
10th–12th Aug	Trenches, Delville Wood, raid
12th Aug	Fricourt
13th–15th Aug	Buire-sur-l'Ancre
15th Aug	By train, Mericourt to Fienvillers
16th Aug	Remaisnil
17th Aug	Lucheux
18th Aug	Souastre
20th–28th Aug	Trenches, Fonquevillers
28th–5th Sept	Reserve, Fonquevillers and Chateau de la Haie
5th–12th Sept	Trenches, Fonquevillers
12th–21st Sept	Reserve, St. Amand
21st–24th Sept	Halloy, Doullens, Remiasnil, Bernatre, Agenvillers
24th–9th Oct	Agenvillers
9th Oct	Maison-Ponthieu
10th Oct	Frohen-le-Grand
11th–19th Oct	Grenas
19th–22nd Oct	Brevillers
22nd Oct	By bus to Coisy
23rd–27th Oct	Daours
27th–30th Oct	Sandpits Camp, Meaulte
30th–2nd Nov	'H' Camp, Carnoy
2nd–5th Nov	Trenches, Gueudecourt
5th–8th Nov	Reserve, Bernafay Wood
8th–10th Nov	Trenches, Gueudecourt, attack 3rd Nov
10th Nov	'H' Camp, Carnoy
11th–14th Nov	Citadel Camp, Fricourt
14th Nov	By train to Hangest
15th–13th Dec	Ailly-sur-Somme
13th Dec	By train, Hangest to Meaulte
14th–23rd Dec	Reserve, Meaulte
23rd–25th Dec	Camp XVIII, Carnoy

25th Dec	Reserve, Guillemont Camp
26th–28th Dec	Trenches, Gueudecourt
28th–31st Dec	Camp XVIII, Carnoy
31st Dec	Reserve, Guillemont
1917	
1st–3rd Jan	Trenches, Sailly-Saillisel
3rd–6th Jan	Camp XVIII, Carnoy
6th–8th Jan	Reserve, Guillemont
8th–10th Jan	Trenches, Cord Trench, Sailly-Saillisel
10th–13th Jan	Camp XVIII, Carnoy
13th Jan	Meaulte
14th–27th Jan	Bonnay
27th–31st Jan	Bronfay Farm, Carnoy
31st–2nd Feb	Support, Fregicourt
2nd–4th Feb	Trenches, Sailly-Saillisel
4th–9th Feb	Support, Fregicourt
9th–12th Feb	Trenches, Sailly-Saillisel
12th–13th Feb	Support, Fregicourt
13th–16th Feb	Reserve, Bronfay Farm, Carnoy
16th–19th Feb	Trenches, Sailly-Saillisel
19th Feb	Support, Fregicourt
20th Feb	Bronfay Farm, Carnoy
21st Feb	By train to Heilly, Franvillers
21st–1st Mar	Franvillers
1st–12th Mar	Puchevillers
13th Mar	Beauval
14th Mar	Bonnieres
15th–22nd Mar	St. Georges
22nd Mar	Villers-l'Hopital
23rd–5th Apr	Sus-St. Leger
5th–8th Apr	Denier
8th Apr	Wanquetin
9th–11th Apr	Arras
12th–18th Apr	Trenches, Feuchy
19th–20th Apr	St. Saveur, Arras
20th–25th Apr	Support, Feuchy
26th Apr	Arras, By bus to Sus-St. Leger

26th–1st May	Sus-St. Leger
1st May	Haute Avesnes
2nd–9th May	Reserve, St. Nicolas, Arras
9th–11th May	Support, Athies
11th–13th May	Trenches and attack, Gavrelle
13th–17th May	Support, Athies
17th–19th May	Reserve, Athies
19th–22nd May	Trenches, Gavrelle
22nd–27th May	Reserve, Athies
27th–29th May	Support, Fampoux
29th May	St. Nicolas, By train to Saulty, Humbercourt
29th–20th June	Humbercourt
20th June	By bus to St. Nicolas
21st–26th June	Support, Fampoux
26th–30th June	Trenches, Chemical Works, Fampoux
1st–3rd July	Reserve, Gavrelle
3rd–7th July	Trenches, Chemical Works, Fampoux
7th–14th July	Reserve, St. Nicolas
15th–20th July	Support, Greenland Hill, Plouvain
20th–23rd July	Trenches, Greenland Hill, Plouvain
23rd–27th July	Support, Gavrelle
27th–31st July	Trenches, Greenland Hill, Plouvain
1st–8th Aug	Reserve, Lichfield Camp, St. Nicolas
8th–12th Aug	Trenches, Chemical Works, Fampoux
12th–16th Aug	Support, Greenland Hill, Plouvain
16th–21st Aug	Trenches, Chemical Works, Fampoux
21st–24th Aug	Support, Greenland Hill, Plouvain
24th–31st Aug	Reserve, St. Nicolas
1st–5th Sept	Trenches, Greenland Hill, Plouvain
5th–10th Sept	Support, Gavrelle
10th–13th Sept	Trenches, Greenland Hill, Plouvain
13th–17th Sept	Support, Gavrelle
17th–22nd Sept	Reserve, St. Nicolas
22nd Sept	Lattre
23rd–4th Oct	Le Souich and Ivergny
5th Oct	By train to Proven
5th–10th Oct	Patiala Camp, Proven

10th–13th Oct	Roussel Camp, Elverdinghe
13th–14th Oct	Support, Pilckem
14th–20th Oct	Boesinghe
20th Oct	Sarawak Camp, St. Sixte, Crombeke
21st Oct	By bus to La Montoire, Nielles-lez-Ardres
24th–6th Nov	Nordausques
6th Nov	By train to Elverdinghe, Marsouin Camp, Pilckem
7th–9th Nov	Trenches, Olga House, Poelcappelle
9th–11th Nov	Reserve, Huddleston Camp, Pilckem
11th–13th Nov	Trenches, Poelcappelle
13th–18th Nov	Reserve, Poussel Farm, Elverdinghe
19th–25th Nov	Support, Whitemill Camp, Langemarck
25th–28th Nov	Support, Langemarck
28th–30th Nov	Trenches, Besace Farm, Poelcappelle
30th–4th Dec	Roussel Farm, Elverdinghe
8th Dec	By train, Proven to Audruicq
9th–12th Dec	Nordausques
12th Dec	Houlle
13th Dec	By train, Arques to Miraumont
14th–17th Dec	Achiet-le-Petit
17th–21st Dec	Rocquigny
21st Dec	Support, Havrincourt
21st–26th Dec	Trenches, Flesquieres
26th–31st Dec	Support, Havrincourt
1918	
1st–4th Jan	Support, Havrincourt
4th–8th Jan	Trenches, Graincourt-lez-Havrincourt
8th–13th Jan	Support, Tank Trench, Gouzeaucourt Wood
13th–18th Jan	Reserve, Saunders Camp, Haplincourt
19th–23rd Jan	Trenches, Hermies
23rd–27th Jan	Reserve, Slag Heap, Canal du Nord, Hermies
27th–31st Jan	Trenches, Graincourt-lez-Havrincourt, raid
1st–6th Feb	Reserve, Hermies
6th–14th Feb	Trenches, Graincourt
14th–18th Feb	Support, Flesquieres
18th–23rd Feb	Reserve, Phipps Camp, Hermies

23rd–24th Feb	Reserve, Bertincourt
24th–2nd Mar	Trenches, Havrincourt
2nd–8th Mar	Support, Havrincourt
8th–17th Mar	Reserve, Hermies
17th–20th Mar	Trenches, Havrincourt
21st Mar	German attack
22nd Mar	Withdrawal to Havrincourt defences
23rd Mar	Further withdrawal to Rocquigny
24th Mar	Attacked, Rocquigny, withdrawal to Le Transloy, Flers and Martinpuich
25th Mar	Withdrawal through Courcelette, Pozieres, Contalmaison, Fricourt to Mametz
26th Mar	Withdrawal through Meaulte and Dernancourt to Henancourt, later Senlis and support, Millencourt
27th Mar	Henencourt and Millencourt
28th Mar	Henencourt
29th–2nd	Apr Line, Albert, co-operated in attack of 50th Brigade, German counter-attack
2nd–4th Apr	Warloy Baillon
4th Apr	Villers Bocage
5th–11th Apr	Havernas
11th–14th Apr	Toutencourt Wood
14th–21st Apr	Reserve, Forceville
21st Apr	In position in Engelbelmer-Millencourt line
22nd–24th Apr	Reserve, Forceville
24th–4th May	Line, Mesnil
4th–7th May	Reserve, Forceville and Engelbelmer
7th–8th May	Reserve, Lealvillers and Forceville
8th May	Camp, Arqueves
9th–18th May	Talmas
18th–25th May	Reserve, Lealvillers
25th–29th May	Support, Mailly-Maillet
29th–6th June	Line, Hamel, German raid
7th–10th June	Support, Auchonvillers
11th–14th June	Reserve, Mailly-Maillet
14th–16th June	Reserve, Acheux Wood

17th–22nd June	Support, Auchonvillers
23rd–10th July	Reserve, Toutencourt Wood
10th–16th July	Line, Bouzincourt, fighting patrol
17th–18th July	Senlis
19th–31st July	Reserve, Engelbelmer
1st Aug	Line, Mesnil and Aveluy Wood
2nd Aug	Enemy withdrawal, patrols pushed forward
3rd Aug	Patrols pushed to Albert-Hamel railway
4th–6th Aug	Line, Mesnil and Aveluy Wood
7th–8th Aug	Reserve, Forceville
9th Aug	Bussy-les-Daours
10th–12th Aug	Heilly
12th Aug	By bus to Hamel, Corbie, reserve, Reginald Wood, Morcourt
12th–15th Aug	Reserve, Reginald Wood, Morcourt
16th Aug	Fouilly, Vecquemont
17th Aug	Vecquemont
18th Aug	Herissart, Beauquesne
19th–20th Aug	Beauquesne
21st Aug	Acheux Wood, Beaussart
21st–23rd Aug	Brown Line, Beaussart
23rd Aug	Support, Hamel
24th Aug	advance to near Courcellette
25th Aug	advance continued, capture of Martinpuich, German counter-attack held-up, Sergeant H J Colley, M.M. won VC
26th Aug	advance to Flers held up, reserve, High Wood
27th–28th Aug	Reserve, High Wood
28th–30th Aug	Reserve, west of Gueudecourt
30th–1st Sept	Line west of Le Transloy, attack on Le Transloy
2nd Sept	Reserve Morval, co-operated in attack on Le Transloy
3rd Sept	Reserve, Rocquigny
4th–6th Sept	Line, Rocquigny
6th Sept	Reserve, Ytres
7th Sept	advance resumed, Dessart Wood, Fins, cleared

9th Sept	attack on Gouzeaucourt, German counter-attack
10th Sept	Support, Equancourt
11th–15th Sept	Reserve, Le Transloy
15th–16th Sept	Reserve, Vallulart Wood, Ytres
16th–17th Sept	Support, south-west of Gouzeaucourt
18th Sept	Second attack on Gouzeaucourt
19th–22nd Sept	Line, Gouzeaucourt
22nd–26th Sept	Reserve, Heudicourt
26th–28th Sept	LesBoeufs
28th–5th Oct	Rocquigny
5th–8th Oct	Equancourt
8th Oct	advance resumed, Gouzeaucourt, Gonnelieu
9th Oct	Mont Ecouvez Farm, Angle Chateau, Selvigny, Sorval Chateau
10th Oct	Montigny, Inchy
11th Oct	Inchy
12th Oct	attack on Neuvilly, Corporal F Lester won VC
13th–17th Oct	reserve, Inchy
17th–20th Oct	Line and attack, Neuvilly
20th–21st Oct	Reserve, Inchy
21st–23rd Oct	Line, Neuvilly
22nd–25th Oct	Audencourt
25th Oct	Beaumont
26th Oct	Ovillers, line, Poix-du-Nord and Englefontaine
26th–29th Oct	Line, Poix-du-Nord and Englefontaine
29th–2nd Nov	Ovillers
2nd Nov	Line, Louvignies
3rd Nov	Assembly positions, Petit Gay Farm, Ghissignies
4th Nov	attack on Futoy and Pont a Vache (Forest of Mormal)
5th–6th Nov	Futoy
7th Nov	through Forest of Mormal to Berlaimont
8th Nov	Auloyne, pursuit of enemy to Beaufort
9th–10th Nov	Outposts, Beaufort
11th Nov	Berlaimont

12th Nov	Through Forest of Mormal to Vendegies-au-Bois
13th–6th Dec	Inchy, inspection By HM King George V on 4th December
6th Dec	Ligny, Harcourt, Lesdain, Masnieres
7th Dec	Marcoing, Flesquieres, Havrincourt, Hermies
8th Dec	Beugny, Fremicourt, Favreuil
9th Dec	Bapaume, Le Sars, Pozieres, Albert
10th Dec	Pont Noyelles, Allonville
11th Dec	Amiens, Ailly-sur-Somme, Picquigny
12th Dec	Soues, Airaines, Vergies
12th–31st Dec	Vergies
1919	
1st Jan–28th Mar	Vergies
29th Mar	Cadre personnel and surplus Officers to Le Quesnoy
31st May	Disbanded

Grandpa joined the 4th King's Liverpool Regiment in February 1919 and stayed until 22nd December 1919

List of Subscribers

Nicholas Wright
Andrew and Anne Wilson
Jane Wilson and Adele
Tom, Poppy and Teddy Wilson
Joe Wilson and Nicole Charlesworth
Matthew Wilson
Daniel Wilson
Anne and David Wright
Gareth Wright
Christopher Escott
Peter Wilson
Marie Wilson
Joanna Kay
Jonathan Kay
Benjamin Kay
Susannah Kay
Terry and Bill Williams
David and Sue Escott
Peter and Wendy Escott
John and Martin Gregson
Michael and Lyn Escott
Stephen and Jill Escott